GW00888896

COLLINS GEM
BASIC FACTS

STUART G. RUDDICK

MATHEMATICS

Christopher Jones BSc
and
Peter Clamp BSc

Revised by
Sheila Cormack MA PhD

COLLINS
London and Glasgow

First published 1982
Revised edition 1988
Reprint 10 9 8 7 6 5 4 3 2

© Wm. Collins Sons & Co. Ltd. 1988

ISBN 0 00 459104 6

Printed in Great Britain

Introduction

Basic Facts is a new generation of illustrated GEM dictionaries in important school subjects. They cover all the important ideas and topics in these subjects up to the level of first examinations.

Bold words in an entry means a word or idea developed further in a separate entry: *italic* words are highlighted for importance.

Symbols in Mathematics

Symbol	Meaning	Example
$=$	equals	$3 = 2 + 1$
$+$	add	$3 + 4 = 7$
$-$	subtract	$3 - 4 = -1$
$\times$	multiply	$3 \times 4 = 12$
$\div$	divide	$3 \div 4 = 0.75$
$\sqrt{}$	square root	$\sqrt{9} = \pm 3$
n	power	$3^2 = 9$
$\angle$	angle	$\angle$ ABC
$\triangle$	triangle	$\triangle$ ABC
$<$	less than	$1 < 4$
$\leqslant$	less than, or equal to	$x \leqslant 4$
$>$	greater than	$6 > 4$
$\geqslant$	greater than, or equal to	$y \geqslant x$
$\neq$	not equal to	$4.9 \neq 49$
$\simeq$	approximately equal to	$3.9 \simeq 4$
∞	proportional to	$x \infty y$
$\{\ \}$	denotes a set	$\{1,2,3,...\}$
ϵ	is a member of	$1 \ \epsilon \ \{1,2,3\}$
$\subset$	is a subset of	$A \subset B$
$\supset$	includes the subset	$B \supset A$
$\mathscr{E}$	universal set	$A \subset \mathscr{E}$
$\varnothing$	empty set	$\{\ \}$
$\cap$	intersection	$A \cap B = \varnothing$
$\cup$	union	$A \cup B = \mathscr{E}$
$\Rightarrow$	implies	$x = 2 \Rightarrow x^2 = 4$
$\therefore$	therefore	
$\equiv$	congruent to	

Abacus A frame containing **parallel** wires carrying beads, used for computation.

beads above bar are worth five times the beads below

Chinese abacus

number shown at the bar is 20675

Abscissa The *x*-**coordinate**, or distance from the *y*-**axis**, of a **point** referred to a system of **Cartesian** coordinates.

y axis

Q (−3, 3)

P (5, 1)

abscissa of Q is −3

abscissa of P is 5

x axis

Absolute The absolute **value** of a **real number** is its numerical value without regard for **sign**. The absolute value of the real number *x* (sometimes called **modulus** or **mod** *x*) is written $|x|$. For example: $|3.6| = 3.6$ and $|-9.1| = 9.1$.

5

Acceleration is rate of change of **velocity** with time.
For example, if a body falls from rest with an acceleration of 9.8 **metres** per **second** per second, its velocity at intervals of a second, from 0 to 3 seconds, would be as shown in the table below:

time (seconds)	0	1	2	3
velocity (metres per second)	0	9.8	19.6	29.4

If **v** is a **vector** representing the velocity of a particle, then the acceleration of the particle is a vector **a** obtained by **differentiating v** with respect to time

$$\mathbf{a} = \frac{d\mathbf{v}}{dt}$$

Acute An acute **angle** is an angle that measures between 0 and 90 **degrees**.

Addition One of the basic **operations** of **arithmetic**. The **sum** of two numbers is determined by the operation addition, which is related to the process of accumulation, for example, 3 + 2 = 5.

In abstract **algebra** used to denote certain operations applied to various **sets**, for example, in the set of 2×2 real **matrices**, addition is defined by:

$$\begin{pmatrix} a & b \\ c & d \end{pmatrix} + \begin{pmatrix} e & f \\ g & h \end{pmatrix} = \begin{pmatrix} a+e & b+f \\ c+d & d+h \end{pmatrix}$$

Affine   An affine **transformation** of the plane is one that can be represented in the form

$$\begin{pmatrix} x \\ y \end{pmatrix} \rightarrow \begin{pmatrix} a & b \\ c & d \end{pmatrix} \begin{pmatrix} x \\ y \end{pmatrix} + \begin{pmatrix} e \\ f \end{pmatrix}$$

Examples include **translations, rotations, shears, reflections**, stretches and **enlargements**.

Under any affine transformation the **images** of **sets** of **parallel lines** are themselves sets of parallel lines.

Algebra   The generalization, and representation in symbolic form, of significant results and patterns in **arithmetic** and other areas of mathematics, for example, $(4 + 3)(4 - 3) = 4^2 - 3^2$ and $(9 + 5)(9 - 5) = 9^2 - 5^2$ are both examples of the algebraic statement $(x + y)(x - y) = x^2 - y^2$.

Algorithm   A standard process designed to solve a particular set of problems.

find d the LCM of x and z	find $q_1 = \dfrac{d}{x}$	find $n_1 = q_1 \times w$	find $q_2 = \dfrac{d}{z}$	find $n_2 = q_2 \times y$	find $n = n_1 + n_2$	result $= \dfrac{n}{d}$

This is the familiar algorithm for the **addition** of **fractions** of the form:

$$\frac{w}{x} + \frac{y}{z}$$

Alternate   Two **angles** are called alternate if they are on opposite sides of a **transversal** cutting two lines, and each has one of the lines for one of its sides.

In the diagram below *a* and *c* are an alternate pair of angles, as are *b* and *d*. Lines PQ and SR are **parallel**, and in this case the alternate pairs of angles are equal. *p* = *r* and *q* = *s*.

Altitude   An altitude of a **triangle** is a **perpendicular** distance from a **vertex** of the triangle to the opposite side of the triangle, called the *base*.

8

In the triangles opposite, AC is the base and the distance BD is the altitude.

The **area** of any triangle can be calculated by $\frac{1}{2} \times$ base length $\times$ altitude.

Note: the three altitudes of any triangle pass through a common point.

Amplitude In an oscillating motion the amplitude is a measure of the maximum **magnitude** of the **displacement** from the **mean** or base position.

For the **periodic function** $f(x) = 3 \sin x$, the amplitude is 3.

Analysis The branch of mathematics concerned with rigorous proofs of propositions mainly in the area of **calculus**.

Angle The angle between two lines is a measure of the inclination of the lines one to the other. Alternatively angle can be viewed as a measure of the **rotation** (about the point of **intersection** of the lines) required to map one line onto the other.

a small angle

a larger angle

The two most common measures of angle are **degree** and **radian** measure.

Annulus An annulus is a **region** of a **plane** bounded by two **concentric circles**.

shaded region is an annulus

If the circles are of **radii** r and R, with $r < R$, then the **area** of the annulus is:

$$\pi R^2 - \pi r^2 \quad \text{or} \quad \pi(R + r)(R - r)$$

Antilogarithm The **inverse** of a **logarithm function**. Used particularly when base 10 logarithms are employed specifically for calculating purposes. For example:

$$\log_{10} 100 = 2 \qquad \text{antilog}_{10} 2 = 100$$

Apex The highest point of a solid or **plane** figure relative to a base plane or line.

11

Approximation An approximation is an inexact result, which is accurate enough for some specific purpose.

For example, to the nearest tenth, the **square root** of 2 is 1.4. To the nearest hundredth it is 1.41.

The study of processes for approximating various forms in mathematics is an important branch of the subject.

For example, *Taylor's Theorem* provides a way of approximating to certain **functions** by **polynomials**.

Newton's method gives an **iterative** way of obtaining approximations to the **roots** of certain **equations**.

Arc An arc is part of a curve.

In particular for the **circle**, the points *A* and *B* define both **minor** and **major** arcs of the circle.

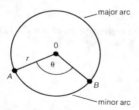

For the minor arc *AB*:

Arc length $= 2\pi r \times \theta/360$, if θ is in **degrees**. Or:
Arc length $= r\theta$, if θ is in **radians**.

Area The measure of the size of a surface. The areas of certain simple figures can be easily calculated.

rectangle:
area = $b \times h$

parallelogram:
area = $b \times h$

trapezium:
area = $\dfrac{a + b}{2} \times h$

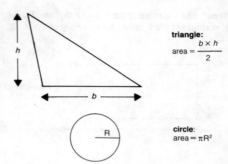

triangle:

$$\text{area} = \frac{b \times h}{2}$$

circle:

$$\text{area} = \pi R^2$$

Argand diagram A rectangular **Cartesian** grid used for diagrammatic representations of **complex numbers**.

The complex number $5 + 2i$ is represented by the point $(5, 2)$.

The horizontal axis is called the real axis, and the vertical axis is called the imaginary axis.

Argument **1.** The argument of a **complex number** is the **angle** between the position **vector** of the number on the **Argand diagram**, and the positive real axis. In the diagram opposite, the argument of the complex number $5 + 2i$ is $21.8°$.

2. The **independent** variable of a function is sometimes called the argument of the function. For example:

x is the argument of the function $y = 3x^2 + 6x - 7$

f is the argument of the function $C = \dfrac{(f - 32) \times 5}{9}$

Arithmetic The study of numbers, particularly with regard to simple operations: addition, subtraction, division and multiplication, and their application to solutions of problems.

(a) **Arithmetic mean** Commonly referred to as the average of a given set of numbers. The arithmetic mean of n numbers $a_1 a_2 \ldots a_n$ is calculated by $(a_1 + a_2 + a_3 + \ldots a_n) \div n$.

For example, the arithmetic mean of 5, 7, 1, 8, 4 is $(5 + 7 + 1 + 8 + 4) \div 5 = 5$.

(b) **Arithmetic progression** A **sequence** in which there is a common difference between any member of the sequence and its successor.

For example, 3, 7, 11, 15, 19, 23 is an arithmetic progression with common difference 4.

Associative Any **binary operation** ∗ which has the property $a * (b * c) = (a * b) * c$ for all members of a, b and c of a given set, is called associative.

Multiplication of real numbers is associative, for example, $8 \times (5 \times 2) = (8 \times 5) \times 2$.

Division is not associative, for example, $80 \div (4 \div 2) \neq (80 \div 4) \div 2$.

Asymptote A line approached, but never reached, by a curve.

The curve of the graph $y = 3 - 1/x$ has the lines $y = 3$ and $x = 0$ as asymptotes. The curve can be drawn as close to $y = 3$ as desired by taking sufficiently large values of x.

Average An average is a single number that represents or typifies a collection of numbers. **Mode**, **mean** and **median** are three commonly used averages.

Axiom A principle, taken to be self-evident, and not requiring proof.

'Things equal to the same thing are equal to each other' is one of the axioms attributed to Euclid.

Axis (plural, axes) An axis is a significant line which a graph, plane shape or solid can be referenced to. For example, **coordinate** axes, axes of **symmetry** etc.

axis of symmetry

coordinate axis

Bar chart A graph using parallel bars to illustrate information. The lengths of the bars are proportional to the quantity represented. Often used to illustrate statistical data.

Base **1.** Number base is the method of grouping used in a number system that relies on place value. In the decimal number system, grouping and place value is based on 10. For example, in base 10, 423 means $3 + (2 \times 10) + (4 \times 100)$. In base 5, 423 would mean $3 + (2 \times 5) + (4 \times 25)$.

2. In expressions like 4^5, 4 is called the base whilst 5 is called the **exponent**. This use of the term base is closely linked to its use in the context of **logarithms**.

In base 10 logarithms $\log 47 = 1.6721$, this means that $10^{1.6721} = 47$.

Bearing is a navigational and surveying term. The bearing of a point A from an observer O is the angle between the line OA and the north line through O, measured in a **clockwise** direction from the north line.

In the diagram the bearing of A from O is 210°. The three figure bearing of O from A is 030°.

Billion A million million (1,000,000,000,000 = 10^{12}). In the U.S.A. it means a thousand million (10^9) and this is becoming the common meaning in Britian.

Bimodal A term used to describe **distributions** of data that show two **modes** or peaks in frequency.

19

percentage of sky covered by cloud

The above distribution is bimodal with modes 0 and 100.

Binary 1. A number system based on grouping in twos. Binary notation requires the use of just two symbols 0 and 1, and its column headings or place values are **powers** of 2:

... 64 32 16 8 4 2 1

Therefore

29 is:				1	1	1	0	1	in binary,
92 is:		1	0	1	1	1	0	0	in binary.

2. A binary **operation** is a rule for combining two **members** of a **set** to produce a third member of the set. The four basic operations of arithmetic — addition,

subtraction, multiplication and division — are examples of binary operations on the set of real numbers.

Binomial A **polynomial** in two variables, for example, $7x + 4y$.

The numbers in the rows of **Pascal's triangle** are called binomial **coefficients**.

$$
\begin{array}{ccccccccccc}
 & & & & & 1 & & & & & \\
 & & & & 1 & & 1 & & & & \\
 & & & 1 & & 2 & & 1 & & & \\
 & & 1 & & 3 & & 3 & & 1 & & \\
 & 1 & & 4 & & 6 & & 4 & & 1 & \\
1 & & 5 & & 10 & & 10 & & 5 & & 1
\end{array}
$$

The numbers in successive rows correspond to the coefficients of the terms when $(x + y)^n$ is expanded in **powers** of x and y for various values of n. For example:

$$(x + y)^5 = x^5 + 5x^4y + 10x^3y^2 + 10x^2y^3 + 5xy^4 + y^5$$

Bisect To bisect is to cut in half. The term is often used in a geometrical context.

21

The line BD bisects $\angle ABC$. The line DE bisects the line AB.

Boundary The boundary of a figure is the curve or curves which define the outer edges of the figure.

The boundary of
a **polygon** consists
of the **edges**.

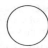

The boundary of
a **circle** is its
circumference.

Brackets Brackets are used to indicate the order in which operations are to be carried out. For example:

$$7 + (2 \times 3) = 7 + 6 = 13 \quad (7 + 2) \times 3 = 9 \times 3 = 27$$

Elementary algebra is often concerned with the introduction or removal of brackets in cases where one operation **distributes** over another. For example:

$$6x^2y + 9xy = 3xy(2x + 3y^2)$$

Calculate To perform a mathematical process, often numerical, to obtain some desired result.

Calculus An important branch of mathematics concerned with the study of the behaviour of functions.
(a) **Differential** calculus is concerned with the variation of functions, with maximum and minimum values, **gradients**, approximations to functions etc.
(b) **Integral** calculus is concerned with calculations of areas and volumes, problems of summation etc.

The techniques of calculus were developed independently by Newton and Leibnitz in the 17th century. Calculus has important applications in many areas of the natural, physical and social sciences.

Cancellation The process of producing, from a given **fraction**, an **equivalent** fraction, by dividing **numerator** and **denominator** by a common **factor**. For example:

$$\frac{15}{20} = \frac{(3 \times 5) \div 5}{(4 \times 5) \div 5} = \frac{3}{4}$$

Cardinal number That aspect of a number that expresses how many elements are in a set. The cardinal number 3 is the property shared by all sets containing three elements.

Cardioid The **locus** of a point on the **circumference** of a circle, which rolls on a fixed circle of equal **radius**.

Cartesian coordinates A method of locating the position of a point on a plane or in space.

In the case of a plane the distances of the point from two perpendicular **axes**, are given as an ordered pair of real numbers (x, y).

The Cartesian coordinates of the points A are (6, 3), see diagram opposite, and (−6, 3), above.

In space, the distances of the point from three mutually perpendicular planes, which in turn form three mutually perpendicular axes, as they intersect in pairs. The distances given as an ordered triple of real numbers (x, y, z).

The Cartesian coordinates of the point B are (3, 4, 5).

Catenary The shape of the curve assumed by a heavy, flexible cable or rope, when suspended from two points.

The graph of $y = \cosh x$ is a catenary.

Centigrade The unit of temperature in which the freezing and boiling temperatures of water are assigned 0 and 100 degrees respectively.

37 degrees centigrade is written 37°C.

Centimetre A centimetre is one-hundredth of a **metre**.

A penny is two centimetres in **diameter**. This is written 2 cm.

Centre The centre of a **circle** is the point equidistant from all points on the **circumference**. The distance from the centre to a point on the circumference is called the **radius** R.

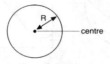

The centre of a **sphere** is the point equidistant from all points on the surface of the sphere. This distance is called the radius of the sphere.

Characteristic When using common, base 10 **logarithms**, the characteristic is the **integer** part of the logarithm when written in the conventional way. The characteristic conveys information regarding the position of the decimal point in the original number. For example:

$$0.041 = 10^{-2} \times 4.1$$
$$\log (0.041) = \log (10^{-2} \times 4.1)$$
$$= \log (10^{-2}) + \log (4.1)$$
$$= -2 + 0.6128$$
$$\text{written } \overline{2}.6128$$

$\overline{2}$ is the characteristic of the logarithm.

Chord A line joining two points on a curve.

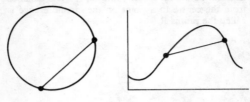

examples of chords

Circle A plane curve formed by the set of all points at a given fixed distance from a fixed point. The fixed point is called the **centre**, and the distance the **radius**.

A circle of radius R has area πR^2 and circumference $2\pi R$.

Circles have line and rotational **symmetry** of infinite order about the centre.

For a fixed **perimeter**, a circle encloses the maximum area for any plane curve.

Circumference Used to mean both the boundary line of a circle and the length of the boundary line, or distance round the circle.

The ratio circumference/**diameter** is a constant for all circles, and is denoted by the Greek letter π (**pi**). Numerically π is an **irrational** number of approximate value 3.14 (to three significant figures). The circumference of a circle may therefore be calculated using the formulae: circumference = π × diameter. For example, for a circle of diameter 6 cm: circumference ≃ 3.14 × 6 cm (≃ 18.8 cm).

Circumscribe A circle is circumscribed to a **polygon** if all the **vertices** of the polygon lie on the circle.

The circumscribed circle to a triangle has its centre at the point of **intersection** of the **perpendicular bisectors** of the sides of the triangle.

A polygon which has a circumscribed circle is called a **cyclic** polygon.

Class interval A grouping of statistical **data** to enable the data to be represented and interpreted in a simpler way.

```
29, 33, 49, 71, 16, 53, 62, 81, 31, 26,
39, 46, 52, 42, 31, 26, 11, 62, 77, 21,
69, 26, 60, 21, 44, 19, 79, 50, 39, 54,
43, 48, 55, 27, 12, 42, 70, 74, 40, 70,
29, 33, 60, 53, 48, 31, 15, 88, 45, 62,
```

For example, the 50 examination percentages could be grouped into the following class intervals:

Mark	1 – 25	26 – 50	51 – 75	76 – 100
Frequency	7	24	15	4

Clockwise An indication of direction of rotation in a plane. A clockwise rotation has the same sense as the rotation of the hands of a clock.

ABC maps to A'B'C' by a clockwise rotation of 90°

Closed **1.** A set is closed under an **operation** when the result of combining together any two members of the set, using the operation, always results in a member of the original set.

For example, the set of **natural** numbers {1, 2, 3, 4, ...} is closed under the operations of addition and multiplication, but is not closed under division or subtraction:

$$3 \div 2 = 1.5, \text{ which is not a natural number}$$
$$1 - 4 = -3, \text{ which is not a natural number}$$

2. A closed curve is one with no end points.

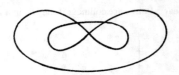

3. A closed interval on the real number line is a set of all numbers x, defined by **inequalities** of the type $a \leqslant x \leqslant b$.

The closed **interval** $\{x: 1 \leqslant x \leqslant 3\}$ is the set of all real numbers between, and including, the 'endpoints' 1 and 3. It is denoted by [1, 3].

Coefficient   1. In simple algebra the coefficient of a term is the numerical part of the term. For example, in $4x^2y + 3xy^2 - 12x + 9y$:

the coefficient of x^2y is 4
the coefficient of xy^2 is 3
the coefficient of x is -12
the coefficient of y is 9

2. In science and engineering the term is often used to denote a specific numerical constant that is characteristic of a particular system, for example, coefficient of linear expansion, coefficient of friction, etc.

Collinear   Points are collinear if they lie in a straight line.

The three points A, B and C are collinear.

Notice the **vectors AB** and **BC** are related: **AB = 2BC**.

32

Notice also that there is a connection between the position vectors of A, B and C:
OB = ⅓**OA** + ⅔**OC** and B divides the line segment **AC** in the **ratio** 2:1.

Column   A vertical array of elements.

The **matrix** $\begin{pmatrix} 6 & 1 & 3 \\ 4 & 2 & 7 \end{pmatrix}$ has three columns.

Combination   A combination from a set of n objects is any selection of n or less objects from the set, regardless of order.

For example, the full list of combinations of three letters from the set $\{a, b, c, d\}$ is: abc, abd, acd, bcd.

The number of combinations of r objects that can be made from a set of n objects is usually denoted by:

$$^nC_r \text{ or } \begin{pmatrix} n \\ r \end{pmatrix}$$

It can be shown that:

$$^nC_r = \frac{n!}{r!(n-r)!} \text{ (where } n! \text{ means \textbf{factorial} } n)$$

For example, $^{12}C_5 = \dfrac{12!}{5! \times 7!} = 792$.

Notice that $^{12}C_5 = {}^{12}C_7$ and in general $^nC_r = {}^nC_{n-r}$.

The values of ^nC_r for varying r are the entries in the appropriate row of **Pascal's triangle**.

33

Common denominator In preparation for the addition or subtraction of **fractions** with unlike **denominators**, the fractions are usually converted into equivalent fractions with the same, or common, denominator.

$$\frac{1}{3} + \frac{1}{2} = \frac{2}{6} + \frac{3}{6} \quad \text{6 is the common denominator}$$

Common difference The difference between successive terms in an **arithmetic progression.** For example:

8, 11, 14, 17, 20   common difference 3
19, 17, 15, 13, 11   common difference -2

Common logarithm **Logarithms** to the **base** of ten are called common logarithms.

Commutative Any operation $*$ which has the property $a * b = b * a$ for all members a and b of a given set, is called commutative.

Multiplication of real numbers is commutative, for example $7 \times 3 = 3 \times 7$.

Subtraction is not commutative, for example, $7 - 3 \neq 3 - 7$.

Complement The complement of a set S is the set consisting of the elements within the **universal set** that are not in S.

The complement of S is usually denoted by S′.

34

The shaded portion of the diagram represents S'.

If $\mathscr{E}$ = {letters of the alphabet}
and C = {consonants}
then C' = {vowels}

Complementary angles Two angles whose sum is
90° are complementary angles.

In the right-angled triangle ABC, ∠BAC and ∠BCA
are complementary angles.

∠BAC is the complement of ∠BCA.

Complete the square A method of solving a quadratic equation by reducing it to the form:

$$(x + h)^2 = k$$

For example:

$$2x^2 + 12x - 3 = 0 \Rightarrow x^2 + 6x - 1.5 = 0$$
$$\Rightarrow x^2 + 6x = 1.5 \Rightarrow (x + 3)^2 - 9 = 1.5$$
$$\Rightarrow (x + 3)^2 = 10.5 \Rightarrow x + 3 = \pm 3.24$$
$$\Rightarrow x = 0.24 \text{ or } x = -6.24$$

Complex numbers An extension of the real number system designed originally to overcome difficulties involving the solution of problems like $x^2 + 3 = 0$, which have no solution in the **real numbers**.

Traditionally complex numbers are written in the form $a + bi$, where a and b are real numbers, and $i^2 = -1$: a and b are called respectively the real and imaginary parts. $x^2 + 3 = 0$ has solutions $x = \sqrt{3}i$ and $x = -\sqrt{3}i$.

To add: $(a + bi) + (c + di) = (a + c) + (b + d)i$.

To multiply:
$(a + bi) \times (c + di) = (ac - bd) + (ad + bc)i$.

Complex numbers have important implications in many branches of pure and applied mathematics.

Component A component of a **vector** is one of a set of two or more, often mutually perpendicular, vectors that together are equivalent in effect to the given vector.

If vector **OA** is of **magnitude** 5 and at 30° to the x-axis then:

Component in the direction of x-axis is vector **OP**.
Magnitude = 5 cos 30° = 4.33.

Component in the direction of y-axis is vector **OQ**.
Magnitude = 5 sin 30° = 2.5.

Composite function The function $f: x \rightarrow (3x + 1)^2$, can be thought of as the composition of two simpler functions:

$$g: x \rightarrow (3x + 1) \text{ and } h: x \rightarrow x^2$$

$$x \xrightarrow{g} (3x + 1) \xrightarrow{h} (3x + 1)^2$$
$$f = hg$$

Notice the notation: $f = hg$ means f is equivalent to the function g followed by h.

Any function that can be split into two or more simpler functions in this way is called a composite function. For example:

if $f:x \rightarrow \sin^2 4x$, then $f = pqr$, where $r:x \rightarrow 4x$, $q:x \rightarrow \sin x$ and $p:x \rightarrow x^2$.

Compound interest A method of calculating **interest** on money where the interest earned during a period is calculated on the basis of the original sum together with any interest earned in previous periods.

£100 invested at 10 per cent per year for three years would appreciate in the following way:

	1st year	2nd year	3rd year
Sum on which interest calculated	£100	£110	£121
Interest (@ 10%)	£ 10	£ 11	£ 12.10
Value of Investment	£110	£121	£133.10

In general if £P is invested at r per cent compound interest, then after n years it would be worth:

$$£P \times \left(\frac{100 + r}{100} \right)^n$$

Computer An electronic device designed to process large amounts of coded information rapidly.

Computer systems commonly comprise three main elements: *Input devices* (for example, keyboard, paper tape etc.) *central processor, output devices* (for example, television monitor, printer, etc.).

Rapid developments in microelectronic technology have resulted in drastic reductions in the size and cost of computers, whilst increasing their processing capabilities.

Concave A concave curve or surface is hollow towards a given point of reference.

The dish of a radio telescope presents a concave surface towards the sky.

Concentric circles Two circles are concentric if they have the same centre but different radii.

Concurrent A number of lines are concurrent if they all meet in a single point. The three **altitudes** of a triangle are concurrent.

Cone A cone is a solid bounded by a **plane** (usually circular) base, and tapering to a fixed point called the **vertex**. A right cone is one in which the axis, or line joining the centre of symmetry of the base to the vertex, is **perpendicular** to the base.

For a cone with a circular base, volume of cone is:

$$V = \tfrac{1}{3}\pi r^2 h$$

where r = base radius, and h = height.

Curved surface area of a right cone is:

$$A = \pi r l$$

where l is the slant height.

Congruent Shapes, plane or solid, are called congruent if they have the same shape and size.

Certain simple transformations such as **rotations**, **reflections** and **translations** map objects onto congruent images.

Conic A curve obtained by taking a plane section through a **cone**.

By varying the angle of cut, four main types of conic can be obtained. See diagram over page.

1. **Circle**. (Cut **parallel** to the base.)
2. **Ellipse**.
3. **Parabola**. (Cut **parallel** to the slant.)
4. **Hyperbola**.

Alternatively a conic can be thought of as the **locus** of a point that moves so that the ratio of its distance from a fixed point (the **focus**) to its distance from a fixed line (the **directrix**) is constant. This ratio is called the **eccentricity** of the conic.

Conjugate   Two angles whose sum is 360° are called conjugate.

The conjugate of the **complex number** $a + bi$ is $a - bi$.

A complex number and its conjugate are related by a **reflection** in the real axis of the **Argand diagram**.

The product of a complex number and its conjugate is equal to the square of its **modulus**

$$(a + bi) \times (a - bi) = a^2 + b^2$$

Constant A fixed quantity in an expression is called a constant.

In the expression $y = 3x + 2$, 3 and 2 are constants whilst x and y are **variables**.

Construction Additional points or lines to supplement a geometrical figure in order to prove some property of the figure are called constructions.

Continuity Quantities like the number of pupils in a class can be measured precisely, and vary in **integer** steps.

class numbers do not vary continuously

When measuring height, however, the result can never be exact. In growing from 160 cm to 161 cm we assume every possible value between 160 and 161 has been attained. See diagram over page.

Quantities such as length, weight, temperature, speed, time, etc., are continuous variables.

43

a person's height is a continuous variable

Converse The converse of the statement 'if a number ends in zero it is divisible by ten' is 'if a number is divisible by ten, then it ends in zero'.

Many important statements in mathematics are in the form 'if x then y'. The converse of such a statement is 'if y then x'.

The converse of a true statement need not itself be true. For example 'if p and q are even, then $p + q$ is even' is a true statement. The converse 'if $p + q$ is even, then p and q are even' is false.

Conversion The process involved in changing from one system (often of units) to another.

For example, to express a temperature, given in the **Fahrenheit** scale, in **centigrade**, use the conversion formula:

$$C = \frac{5}{9} (F - 32)$$

Convex A curve or surface that bulges towards a given point of reference is called convex.

44

The dome of St. Paul's Cathedral presents a convex surface to the sky.

A convex figure is one in which any line joining two points on the figure is contained within the figure.

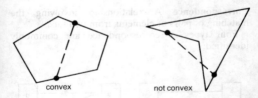

convex   not convex

Coordinates A coordinate system is used to locate points on a plane or in space. **Cartesian** and **polar** are two commonly used coordinate systems.

Coplanar Sets of points or lines lying in the same **plane** are called coplanar.

45

Correlation A statistical term used to describe a relationship between two varying quantities, when changes in one variable are linked to changes in the other. A positive correlation occurs when increases and decreases in the two variables happen together. A negative correlation occurs when increases in one variable are associated with decreases in the other.

Doctors, for example, have suggested a positive correlation between the habit of cigarette smoking and the incidence of heart disease.

A correlation coefficient is a number between -1 and 1, that gives a measure of correlation between the values of two variables.

Correspondence A relationship involving the matching of pairs of elements from two sets.

Four types of correspondence are commonly identified:

one to one
correspondence

one to many
correspondence

many to one
correspondence

many to many
correspondence

Corresponding points, lines and angles When two figures are related by a simple **transformation**, features of the first figure are said to correspond to their images on the transformed figure.

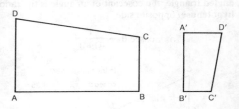

ABCD and A'B'C'D' are **similar quadrilaterals**, C and C' are corresponding points, ∠ DAB and ∠ D'A'B' are corresponding angles.

When a **transversal** cuts a pair of lines, as in the diagram over page, the pairs of angles, p and p', q and q', r and r', s and s' are called corresponding angles.

47

If the pair of lines cut by the transversal are **parallel**, the corresponding angles are equal.

Cosecant A trigonometric function. In a **right-angled** triangle, the cosecant of an angle is the ratio, **hypotenuse**/opposite side.

$$\text{cosec } \theta = \frac{1}{\sin \theta}$$

in the triangle ABC
$$\text{cosec } \theta = \frac{AC}{BC} = \frac{5}{4} = 1.25$$

The value of θ can now be determined by examining a table of values for the cosecant function. $\theta = 53.1°$.

48

Cosine A trigonometric function. In a **right-angled** triangle the cosine of an angle is the ratio, adjacent side/**hypotenuse**.

in the triangle ABC
$$\cos \theta = \frac{CB}{CA} = \frac{5}{13} = 0.385$$

The value of θ can now be determined by examining a table of values for the cosine function. $\theta = 67.4°$.

in the triangle PQR
$$\cos 60° = \frac{PQ}{PR}$$

In the triangle PQR above:

$$\cos 60° = \frac{PQ}{PR}$$

From the table of values for the cosine function, $\cos 60° = 0.5$. Hence:

$$0.5 = \frac{PQ}{9.6} \quad \text{and} \quad PQ = 4.8$$

49

Cotangent A trigonometric function. In a **right-angled** triangle the cotangent of an angle is the ratio, adjacent side/opposite side.

in the triangle ABC

$$\cot \theta = \frac{BC}{BA} = \frac{8}{6} = 1.33$$

The value of θ can now be determined by examining a table of values for the cotangent function. θ = 36.9°.

Count To count the number of objects in a **set** is to match the objects in a one-to-one fashion with the names of the positive **integers** – 'one, two, three . . .'

The positive integers or natural numbers are often called counting numbers.

Cross multiply A term used to describe a process of simplifying equations involving fractional terms. For example:

If $\frac{4x}{3} = 6$, then $x = \frac{6 \times 3}{4}$ so $x = 4\frac{1}{2}$.

Cross section The cross section of a solid is the plane shape that results from cutting through the solid, often at right angles to an **axis of symmetry** of the solid.

cross section of a tree trunk

cross section of a girder

Cube **1.** A regular solid with six square faces.

a die

sugar cubes

2. To cube a number is to raise the number to the **power** of three. 'Four cubed' is written

$$4^3 = 4 \times 4 \times 4 = 64.$$

Cubic A cubic function is a **polynomial** of the third **degree**:

$$ax^3 + bx^2 + cx + d$$

All cubic equations with real **coefficients** have at least one real solution.

The cubic **metre**, cubic **centimetre**, etc., are units used in measuring volume. A solid with volume three cubic metres, written 3 m³, has the same volume as three cubes each with 1 m edges.

Cuboid A cuboid is a solid with six **rectangular** faces, the opposite faces being equal in size.

Cumulative frequency In **statistics** a method of grouping **frequencies** of the value of some **variable** by adding the frequencies not greater than certain values of the variable.

Frequency table for pupils' marks in a test.	
mark	frequency
0	4
1	5
2	8
3	12
4	10
5	3

Cumulative frequency table for same marks.	
mark	cumulative frequency
⩽0	4
⩽1	9
⩽2	17
⩽3	29
⩽4	39
⩽5	42

A cumulative frequency graph is called an **ogive**.

Cusp A simple cusp is a point on a curve where the curve turns back on itself, and where the two branches of the curve share a common **tangent**, the branches being on opposite sides of the tangent. For example, $y^2 = x^3$.

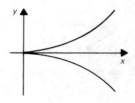

The curve above has a simple cusp at the origin, where the x-axis is the common tangent.

Cyclic A cyclic **permutation** of an ordered set is achieved by mapping each object to its successor, the last object being mapped to the first. For example:

$$(1, 2, 3) \rightarrow (2, 3, 1) \rightarrow (3, 1, 2)$$

The first permutation is denoted by:

$$\begin{pmatrix} 1 & 2 & 3 \\ 2 & 3 & 1 \end{pmatrix}.$$

A cyclic **quadrilateral** is a four-sided plane shape having **vertices** lying on the **perimeter** of a circle.

The opposite angles of a cyclic quadrilateral are **supplementary**.

Cycloid A cycloid is the curve traced by a point P on the **circumference** of a circle which rolls along a straight line.

For a circle of radius a the parametric (see **Parameter**) equation of a cycloid is:

$$x = a(\theta - \sin \theta) \quad y = a(1 - \cos \theta)$$

54

Cylinder A cylinder is a solid with one **axis of symmetry** about which it has a uniform circular **cross section**.

The volume of a cylinder is given by:

$V = \pi r^2 h$ (The area of a circular end multiplied by the height.)

The curved surface area of a cylinder is given by:

$A = 2\pi rh$ (The **circumference** of a circular end multiplied by the height.)

Data Information often in numerical form, which has been collected for **statistical** purposes.

Decagon A decagon is a **polygon** with ten sides.

Decimal A general term applied to the system of representing whole and fractional numbers in the **base** of ten.

A decimal fraction is one with **denominator** being a power of ten, for example, $^3/_{10}$, $^7/_{100}$, $^{38}/_{1000}$, etc.

The base 10 place value system for whole numbers is extended in the decimal system to include the representation of decimal fractions.

$$13\,\frac{17}{100} = 13.17$$

tens tenths
units hundredths

The decimal point is used to identify place values as indicated above.

All **rational numbers** can be represented in decimal form by a **terminating** or **recurring** sequence of decimal **digits**.

Irrational numbers can be represented **approximately** in decimal form by **rounding off** to a prescribed number of decimal places. For example:

$$\sqrt{2} = 1.41 \text{ to 2 decimal places}$$
$$\sqrt{2} = 1.4142 \text{ to 4 decimal places}$$
$$\pi = 3.142 \text{ to 3 decimal places.}$$

Degree 1. A unit for measuring angles, in which one complete rotation is divided into 360 degrees (written 360°).

a right angle contains 90°

a straight angle contains 180°

2. The degree of a **polynomial** expression or equation of one variable is the highest power to which the unknown is raised. For example:

$7x^5 - 5x^3 + 19x^2 - 3$ is of degree 5 in x.

An expression in several variables, for example:

$$8x^3y^2z^4$$

is said to be of degree 9 (the sum of the powers of x, y and z), but of degree 2 in y.

Denominator The 'bottom number' of a **fraction**. For example, the denominator of $^3/_4$ is 4.

Depression The angle of depression of an object from an observer viewing the object from above, is the angle between the line joining the object and the observer, and the horizontal plane.

The angle of depression from the lighthouse to the ship is 20°.

Derivative If $y = f(x)$ is a **function** of the **variable** x, the derivative of $y = f(x)$ at some $x = a$, is the rate of change of the function with respect to x at a. It is found by **differentiation**.

The derivative is often interpreted as the slope of the graph of $y = f(x)$ at $x = a$.

The derivative of $y = f(x)$ is usually written dy/dx or $f'(x)$. For $f(x) = x^3$, $f'(x) = 3x^2$, thus the rate of change of x^3 at $x = 4$ is $3 \times 4^2 = 48$.

Determinant The determinant of a square **matrix M** is a number associated with that matrix.

For the 2×2 matrix $M = \begin{pmatrix} a & b \\ c & d \end{pmatrix}$ it is written

$$\begin{vmatrix} a & b \\ c & d \end{vmatrix} \quad \text{or Det M, and is equal to } ad - bc.$$

The determinants of larger matrices can be evaluated in a similar way. For example.

$$\begin{vmatrix} a & b & c \\ d & e & f \\ g & h & i \end{vmatrix} = a \begin{vmatrix} e & f \\ h & i \end{vmatrix} - b \begin{vmatrix} d & f \\ g & i \end{vmatrix} + c \begin{vmatrix} d & e \\ g & h \end{vmatrix}$$

The theory of determinants is particularly useful in the application of matrices to solving sets of **linear** equations, and linear transformations.

Diagonal A diagonal of a **polygon** is a line joining any two non-adjacent **vertices**.

diagonal of a square

diagonals of a **hexagon**

An n sided polygon has $n - 3$ diagonals from any vertex, and $\frac{1}{2}n(n - 3)$ distinct diagonals in total.

Diameter The diameter of a circle is a **chord** that passes through the centre of the circle.

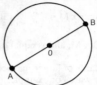

If 0 is the centre of the circle then AB is a diameter of the circle.

The length of the diameter of a circle is twice the length of the **radius** of the circle.

Difference The difference between two numbers a and b is the result obtained by subtracting one from the other, i.e. $a - b$.

The difference of two squares $a^2 - b^2$ is the common name given to the factorization
$a^2 - b^2 = (a - b)(a + b)$.

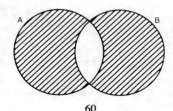

The symmetric difference of two sets A and B is $(A \cap B') \cup (B \cap A')$ or $(A \cup B) \cap (A \cap B)'$ and is represented by the shaded area on the **Venn diagram** above.

Differentiation The process of finding the **derivative** $f'(x)$ of a function f.

Essentially the process involves the evaluation of:

$$\text{Limit } \frac{f(x + h) - f(x)}{h} \text{ as } h \text{ tends to } 0.$$

This may be viewed as finding the **gradient** of the **tangent** to the graph of f at the point x, by taking the limit of the gradients of a sequence of **chords** over increasingly small intervals.

For many families of functions, derivatives are simply deducible from the form of the original function. For example:

For $f(x) = Ax^n$, $f'(x) = nAx^{n-1}$
So, if $f(x) = 3x^3 + 2x^2 + 1$ then $f'(x) = 9x^2 + 4x$.

Digit A single numeral (0, 1, 2, . . . 9) when used as part of the representation of a number in a place-value system of writing numbers is called a digit. For example 35780 — this number has five digits, the first being 3, and the last 0.

Digital A digital computer is one that represents numbers by a digital code (usually of ones and zeros), rather than by a continuously measurable quantity as do analogue devices.

Directed numbers Signed numbers (positive and negative) in which positive numbers are represented along a line relative to an origin 0, and negative numbers are similarly represented in the reverse direction.

$$\ldots \quad -3 \quad -2 \quad -1 \quad 0 \quad +1 \quad +2 \quad +3 \quad +4 \quad \ldots$$

In the directed number model, -3 can be thought of in two ways either as a position on the number line, or as a vector shift of 'three units left' along the line. Directed numbers can be used as a model for operations with **integers**. For example, $+1 + -3 = -2$ might be viewed as 'one step right then three steps left gives two steps left'.

Directrix A line that defines the shape of a curve of the **conic** family. For any point on a given curve the ratio of its distance from a fixed point (**focus**) to the directrix line is constant.

Discrete Quantities that can be measured by a counting process are called discrete. Discrete variables change in a discontinuous way.

The number of trees in a plantation is a discrete variable over a given period of time.

The height of a particular tree in the plantation is not a discrete variable — it is **continuous**.

63

Discriminant For a **quadratic equation** such as $ax^2 + bx + c = 0$ the quantity $b^2 - 4ac$ is called the discriminant.

If: $b^2 - 4ac > 0$ the equation has two real **roots**
$\quad b^2 - 4ac = 0$ the equation has coincidental real roots
$\quad b^2 - 4ac < 0$ the equation has **complex** roots

Disjoint Two **sets** are disjoint if their **intersection** is the **empty set**. If A = {odd numbers} and B = {even numbers} then A and B are disjoint.

Displacement A displacement is a **vector** quantity representing a change of position.

The displacement from A(2,2) to B(5,4) can be represented by the vector $\begin{pmatrix} 3 \\ 2 \end{pmatrix}$ and is of **magnitude** 3.61 at 33.7° to the x-axis.

64

Distribution The set of values and associated **frequencies** of a **statistical** variable is called a distribution.

In throwing a die the number of sixes has a binomial distribution:

Number of sixes obtained in 10 throws of a die	Relative frequency
0	0.16
1	0.32
2	0.29
3	0.16
4	0.05
5	0.01
more than 6	0.01

65

Statistical data such as the height of the girls in a class often has a *normal* distribution:

Relative frequency

height

The normal distribution is **symmetric** about the **mean**.

The number of telephone calls per minute passing through an exchange has a *Poisson* distribution:

Relative frequency

number of calls per minute

The Poisson distribution is **skew-symmetric**.

Distributive law When two **binary** operations $\oplus$ and $*$ are defined on a set S, and for any three elements x, y, z in S

$$x * (y \oplus z) = (x * y) \oplus (x * z)$$

$*$ is said to distribute over $\oplus$.

In the arithmetic of real numbers multiplication distributes over addition. For example:

$$7 \times (4 + 3) = (7 \times 4) + (7 \times 3)$$

Addition does not, however, distribute over multiplication. For example:

$$5 + (3 \times 6) \neq (5 + 3) \times (5 + 6)$$

Dividend A number that is to be divided by another. For example, in $2468 \div 3$, 2468 is the dividend.

Division The **inverse** operation to multiplication. One of the basic operations of arithmetic. The **quotient** of two numbers is determined by this operation which is associated with the process of dividing one quantity into a number of equal parts.

Divisor In a **division** problem the quantity by which the **dividend** is to be divided is called the divisor. The **factors** of a whole number are sometimes called divisors. For example, in $2468 \div 3$, 3 is the divisor.

Dodecagon A **polygon** having 12 sides, and hence 12 interior angles, is called a dodecagon.

Dodecahedron A **polyhedron** having 12 faces is called a dodecahedron.

A **regular** dodecahedron has for its faces 12 regular **pentagons**.

a regular
dodecahedron

Domain The set which acts as inputs to a **function** is called the domain of the function. For example, for the function of $y = \sqrt{x}$, the domain is normally taken to be the set of possible values of the **variable** x, i.e., non-negative real numbers.

Dual In plane and solid geometry figures that can be obtained from one another by interchanging particular elements (for example, points ↔ lines) are called dual figures.

Theorems proved about one figure provide analogous theorems about the dual.

Duodecimal The number system employing the **base** of 12 is called the duodecimal system.

Two extra **numerals** more than the familiar 0, 1,

68

2, ... 9 are needed to represent 10 and 11 in this system.

Base 10		Duodecimal	
41	↔	35	

tens units   twelves units

If T and E are taken as symbols for 10 and 11 respectively then:

Base 10		Duodecimal
22	↔	1T
35	↔	2E
41	↔	35

tens units   twelves units

e The symbol given to the **irrational** number which is the base of the natural **logarithm** function. A fundamental constant of both mathematics and the physical world.

e = limit of $(1 + 1/n)^n$ as n increases. To ten places of decimals $e \simeq 2.7182818284$.

A unique property of the function $y = e$ is that the gradient of its graph for any value of x is identical to the value of the function for that value, i.e.

$$\frac{dy}{dx} = y$$

Thus the size of any quantity that grows or decays at a rate **proportional** to its size at a given time is related to the number e.

69

Eccentricity For a **conic**, the ratio *e* of the distance of any point on the curve from the **focus** to the distance of the same point from the **directrix**, is called the eccentricity.

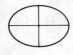

For *e* < 1 the conic is an **ellipse**

e < 1

For *e* = 1 the conic is a **parabola**

e = 1

For *e* > 1 the conic is a **hyperbola**

e > 1

Edge A line forming the intersection of two faces of a **polyhedron** or other solid is called an edge.

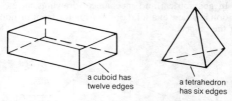

a cuboid has twelve edges

a tetrahedron has six edges

Element The individual members of a **set** are called its elements. For example:

Red is an element of the set of primary colours.
7 is an element of the set of odd numbers.
The symbol **∈** means 'is an element of' in set notation, hence 7 **∈** {odd numbers}.

Elevation The angle of elevation of an object from an observer viewing the object from below, is the angle between the line joining the object and the observer, and the horizontal plane.

25°

The angle of elevation of the plane from the radar station is 25°.

In geometrical and mechanical drawings an elevation is a view of a solid object from the front or side of the object.

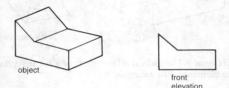

object

front
elevation

Ellipse A plane curve belonging to the **conic** family. An ellipse has an **eccentricity** e of less than 1.

If a **cone** is cut by a plane to form a **cross section** which is a **closed curve**, the cross section is an ellipse.

An ellipse can also be thought of as the **locus** of a point in a plane that moves such that the sum of the distances of the point from two fixed points, called the **foci**, is constant.

An ellipse has two **axes** of symmetry called the major and minor axes.

For any point P
AP + BP = 2a

For an ellipse with major axis extending from $(-a, 0)$ to $(a, 0)$, and minor axis from $(0, -b)$ to $(0, b)$ the **Cartesian equation** is:

$$\frac{x^2}{a^2} + \frac{y^2}{b^2} = 1$$

The foci are at $(c, 0)$ and $(-c, 0)$ where $c^2 = a^2 - b^2$ and the **directrices** are the lines

$$x = \frac{a^2}{c} \quad \text{and} \quad x = -\frac{a^2}{c}$$

A circle is a particular case of an ellipse where $e = 0$.
The area enclosed by an ellipse is equal to πab.

73

Empty set The empty set, which is denoted by the symbol ø, is a set which contains no members. For example, the set of female kings of England = ø.

Enlargement An enlargement is a **transformation** of plane or solid shapes in which shapes are mapped onto **similar** shapes using a centre of enlargement.

$$\frac{A'B'}{AB} = \frac{B'C'}{BC} = \frac{A'C'}{AC}$$

$$\frac{OB'}{OB} = \frac{OA'}{OA} = \frac{OC'}{OC}$$

The **scale factor** of an enlargement is the ratio of corresponding lengths on the object to those on the **image**. Alternatively the scale factor can be viewed as the ratio of distances between the centre and the object and corresponding distances between the centre and the image.

Enlargements centred at the origin can be represented in **matrix** form. For example: in a plane

$$\begin{pmatrix} 3 & 0 \\ 0 & 3 \end{pmatrix} \text{ scale factor 3}$$

$$\begin{pmatrix} -2 & 0 \\ 0 & -2 \end{pmatrix}$$ scale factor 2 with a reflection in the centre

Envelope A plane curve which is **tangential** to each member of a whole family of curves.

Here the family of curves is of circles of radius *a* whose centres are all distance *b* from a fixed point 0.

This family has two envelopes, themselves circles, one of radius $(b + a)$ and the other of radius $(b - a)$.

Epicycloid An epicycloid is the path traced by a

point P on the **circumference** of a circle which itself rolls on the circumference of another circle.

An epicycloid forms 'arches' around the fixed circle. If the radii of the rolling and fixed circles are *a* and *b* respectively, the curve has *n* 'arches' when *b* = *na*.

Equal Quantities which are alike in certain respects are said to be equal in those respects. The symbol = is used to denote equality.

The relationship of equality is an example of an **equivalence** relation.

Equation An equation is a statement of an equality relationship between two quantities or expressions. A large part of mathematics is concerned with the study of methods of solution for various types of equations. For example:

$$(x + 1)^2 = x^2 + 2x + 1$$

is an equation expressing an identity relationship which holds for any numerical value of *x*.

$$3x + 1 = 10$$

is a simple **linear** equation which is conditional upon the value of *x*.

The solution of this equation is *x* = 3.

Other examples of common types of simple equations include **quadratic** and **simultaneous equations**.

Equator A line of **latitude** which is a great circle.

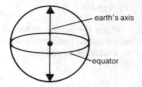

The equator is the circle produced on the earth's surface by taking a section through the centre of the earth, perpendicular to the earth's axis.

The equator is the reference line for positions of latitude on the earth's surface. For example, latitude 60° north means 60° north of the equator.

Equilateral An equilateral **polygon** is one with all its sides equal in length.

an equilateral pentagon

an equilateral triangle

An equilateral triangle also necessarily has equal interior angles. This is however not generally true of all equilateral polygons.

Equilibrium When the system of forces acting on a body are balanced and have a zero **resultant**, the body is said to be in a state of equilibrium.

This marble, balanced on an upturned cup, is in a state of *unstable* equilibrium. When displaced the marble will move away from the position of equilibrium.

This marble resting in the cup is in a state of *stable* equilibrium. When displaced the marble will move back to the position of equilibrium.

Equivalence An equivalence **relation** R between the members of a set has three properties:

(a) It is **reflexive**: cRc for all elements c in the set.
(b) It is **symmetric**: If aRb then bRa.
(c) It is **transitive**: If dRe and eRf then dRf.

For example, the relation 'is **similar** to' defined on a set of plane figures is an equivalence relation.

An equivalence relation splits up a set into distinct subsets called *equivalence classes*.

Equivalent Two **fractions** are called equivalent if they represent the same **rational** number, that is, they can be **cancelled** to produce a common fraction.

The fractions a/b and c/d are equivalent when $ad = bc$.

For example, $^3/_4$, $^6/_8$, $^9/_{12}$, $^{21}/_{28}$ and $^{315}/_{420}$ are all equivalent.

Euclidean After the famous Greek mathematician Euclid. A term often used to describe the geometry of ordinary space of two or three dimensions.

Euler's formula

For **networks**

$$nodes + regions = arcs + 2$$

4 nodes
4 regions
6 arcs

79

For **polyhedra**

faces + vertices = edges + 2

5 faces
5 vertices
8 edges

Even Numbers that have 2 as a **factor** are called even. Even numbers are the multiples of 2: 2, 4, 6, 8 ...

Expansion The extended or expanded form of an expression. For example, the expansion of $(x + 1)^3$ is $x^3 + 3x^2 + 3x + 1$.

Exponent An exponent is the numerical symbol used to indicate the raising of a **base** number to some indicated **power**. For example, the exponent in 3^4 is 4.

Exponential A term applied to functions of the type $f(x) = a^x$. All functions of this type have certain features in common. For example, they are positive for all x. They tend to 0 as x becomes increasingly negative. Their graphs cut the y-axis at 1, that is, $f(0) = 1$.

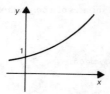

The function $f(x) = e^x$, in particular, is known as the exponential function. These functions are associated with situations of natural growth and decay. Their inverses are **logarithmic** functions.

Extrapolate The use of past figures to try and predict the future is called extrapolation. In the graph below we try to predict the population of Great Britain in 1911 from the figures over the period 1821–91.

Face The flat surfaces of a **polyhedron** are called its faces.

this pyramid has four faces

a cube has six faces

Factor The factors of a number are all numbers which divide into it exactly. For example:

> factors of 12 are 1, 2, 3, 4, 6, 12
> factors of 17 are 1, 17
> factors of 32 are 1, 2, 4, 8, 16, 32

The factors of a **polynomial** are other polynomials that divide into it exactly. For example:

> factors of $x^3 - 8$ are $x - 2$ and $x^2 + 2x + 4$
> factors of $x^3 + 1$ are $x + 1$ and $x^2 - x + 1$

Factor theorem The factor theorem states that if $P(x)$ is a **polynomial** and $P(a) = 0$, then $x - a$ is a **factor** of the polynomial. For example:

if $P(x) = x^3 - 6x^2 + 11x - 6$
$P(1) = 1 - 6 + 11 - 6 = 0 \Rightarrow x - 1$ is a factor
$P(2) = 8 - 24 + 22 - 6 = 0 \Rightarrow x - 2$ is a factor
$P(3) = 27 - 54 + 33 - 6 = 0 \Rightarrow x - 3$ is a factor

so the factors of $x^3 - 6x^2 + 11x - 6$ are $(x - 1)$, $(x - 2)$ and $(x - 3)$ and
$x^3 - 6x^2 + 11x - 6 \equiv (x - 1)(x - 2)(x - 3)$.

Factorial Factorial n, written as $n!$ is defined as the product of all the integers 1, 2, 3, ... up to and including n. For example:

$$5! = 5 \times 4 \times 3 \times 2 \times 1 = 120$$
$$4! = 4 \times 3 \times 2 \times 1 \qquad = 24$$
$$3! = 3 \times 2 \times 1 \qquad = 6$$
$$2! = 2 \times 1 \qquad = 2$$
$$1! = 1 \qquad = 1$$

Using the above pattern, we may deduce a value of 1 for $0! = 1$.

Factorize To factorize a number or **polynomial** is to express it as the product of some of its **factors**.

For example:

$$12 = 6 \times 2 = 4 \times 3 = 2 \times 2 \times 3,$$
$$125 = 5^3 = 5 \times 25,$$
$$x^3 - 8 = (x - 2)(x^2 + 2x + 4),$$
$$x^3 - 2x^2 + x = x(x - 1)^2.$$

Fahrenheit The Fahrenheit scale is a scale of measurement of temperatures. In this system, the boiling and freezing points of water are 212° and 32° respectively. The normal body temperature of a person is 98.4° Fahrenheit.

A temperature in Fahrenheit may be changed to a temperature in **centigrade**, the other common scale of measurement, using the formula:
$$C = 5/9 \ (F - 32).$$

Fibonacci The Fibonacci sequence of numbers is the sequence, 1, 1, 2, 3, 5, 8, 13, 21, 34, etc. Each member of the sequence is the sum of the two preceding numbers.

Flowchart A diagram showing the procedure to be followed in solving a problem. For example, an **iterative** way of finding $\sqrt[3]{10}$ is shown by the flowchart below.

84

Focus   A point associated with a curve of the **conic** family. For any point on a conic curve, the ratio of the distance of the point from the focus to its distance from the **directrix** line is a constant (called the **eccentricity**).

Foot   A unit of length. 1 foot is equal to 12 **inches** or just over 30 **centimetres**.

Formula   A general rule or result stated in algebraic equation form.
Examples:

$P = 2(l + w)$ is a formula for the **perimeter** of a **rectangle**, l and w stand for the length and width of the rectangle.

$F = 9/5\ C + 32$ is a formula linking temperatures in degrees **Fahrenheit** (F) and **centigrade** (C).

$A = \pi R^2$ is a formula for the area of a circle in terms of its radius R.

In the above examples the letters P, F and A are said to be the *subjects* of the formulae. We may change the subject by rearranging the formula. For example:

$$P = 2(l + w) \qquad\qquad A = \pi R^2$$

$$\frac{P}{2} = l + w \qquad\qquad \frac{A}{\pi} = R^2$$

$$\frac{P}{2} - l = w \qquad\qquad \sqrt{\frac{A}{\pi}} = R$$

w is now the subject $\qquad$ R is now the subject

85

Fraction A fraction is part of a whole. The fraction 'three quarters' is denoted by the **rational number** $^3/_4$. The bottom number is called the **denominator** and the top number is called the **numerator**.

The shaded part represents $^5/_8$ of the whole circle, since the circle has been divided into eight equal parts, five of which are shaded.

addition:
$$4^5/_8 + 3^7/_{12} = 7\frac{15 + 14}{24} = 7^{29}/_{24} = 8^5/_{24}$$

subtraction:
$$4^3/_8 - 1^7/_{12} = 3_2\frac{\overset{24}{9} - 14}{24} = 2^{19}/_{24}$$

multiplication:
$$3^3/_4 \times 1^1/_9 = \frac{^5 15}{4_2} \times \frac{^5 10}{9_3} = \frac{25}{6} = 4^1/_6$$

division:
$$3^3/_4 \div 1^1/_9 = \frac{15}{4} \div \frac{10}{9} = \frac{^3 15}{4} \times \frac{9}{10_2} = \frac{27}{8} = 3^3/_8$$

86

A fraction may be changed into a **decimal** by dividing the numerator by the denominator. For example:

$$\frac{3}{8} = 0.375 \qquad \begin{array}{r} 0.375 \\ 8\overline{)3.0^60^40} \end{array}$$

Frequency The frequency of an event is how many times it has occurred. For example, a die is thrown ten times and the results are 1, 2, 5, 6, 5, 4, 3, 1, 2, 1. The frequency of 1 is three since three of the throws were 1s. The results may be written in a frequency table as below:

Score	1	2	3	4	5	6
Number of throws (frequency)	3	2	1	1	2	1

The relative frequency of 5 is

$$\frac{\text{frequency of 5}}{\text{total number of throws}} = 0.2$$

Frustum The frustum of a solid shape is any part of the solid contained between two parallel planes that cut the solid.

frustum of a cone

frustum of a pyramid

Function A function is a relation between two sets called the **domain** and **range** in which each member of the domain is related to precisely one member of the range, called its **image**.

For a function f and element x in the domain of f, the image of x is denoted by $f(x)$. x and $y = f(x)$ are **variables**. For example:

$x \rightarrow 2x + 3$ Describes a function from the set of **real numbers** to itself.

$x \rightarrow$ 'Number of factors of x' describes a function from the set of positive **integers** to itself.

$x \rightarrow 1/x$ Describes a function from the set of non-zero real numbers (0 would have no image) to itself.

Gallon A measure of volume. There are 8 **pints** in 1 gallon. 1 gallon is approximately 4.5 **litres**.

Geometric mean The geometric mean of a set of n numbers is the nth **root** of the **product** of all of the numbers. For example:

geometric mean of 2, 4, 8 is $\sqrt[3]{2 \times 4 \times 8} = \sqrt[3]{64} = 4$

geometric mean of 2, 3, 6, 12, 18, is

$$\sqrt[5]{2 \times 3 \times 6 \times 12 \times 18} = 6$$

Geometric progression A geometric progression is a **sequence** of numbers, in which each term is a constant **multiple** of the preceding term. This multiple is called the *common ratio*. For example:

2, 6, 18, 54, 162 common ratio is 3
64, 32, 16, 8, 4, 2 common ratio is $\frac{1}{2}$
$\frac{1}{4}$, −1, 4, −16, 64 common ratio is −4

The sum of the terms of the general geometric progression $a + ar + ar^2 + ar^3 \ldots + ar^{n-1}$ is given by the formula:

$$S_n = \frac{a(r^n - 1)}{r - 1} \quad \text{or} \quad \frac{a(1 - r^n)}{1 - r}$$

(a is the first term of the series and r is the common ratio).

The sum of an infinite geometric progression can be calculated if the common ratio is between -1 and $+1$.

$$S_\infty = \frac{a}{1 - r}$$

Geometry Geometry is a branch of mathematics which involves the study of properties of points, lines and planes and of curves, shapes and solids.

Glide reflection A geometrical **transformation** of the plane composed of a **reflection** and a **translation**.

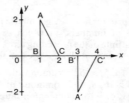

$\triangle A'B'C'$ is obtained from $\triangle ABC$ by a glide reflection in the x-axis. In **vector** notation:

$$\begin{pmatrix} x \\ y \end{pmatrix} \rightarrow \begin{pmatrix} x + 2 \\ -y \end{pmatrix}$$

Gradient The gradient of a line is a measure of its steepness.

The gradient is $^4/_2 = 2$. Lines sloping this way have a positive gradient.

The gradient is $^{-5}/_2 = -2^1/_2$. Lines sloping this way have a negative gradient.

tangent to curve at point P

gradient at P $= \frac{4}{8} = \frac{1}{2}$

91

The gradient of a curve at a particular point is the gradient of the **tangent** drawn to the curve at that point. The curve $y = f(x)$ has gradient $f'(x)$.

Gram A unit of mass. There are one thousand grams in a **kilogram** (1000 g = 1 kg), and just over 28 grams in 1 **ounce**. 1 **cubic centimetre** of water has a mass of 1 gram.

Graph A graph is a diagramatic representation of the relationship between various quantities.

Often, **coordinates** and **axes** are used.

Great circle A great circle is a circle drawn on the earth's surface that has the same **radius** as that of the earth. For example, the **equator** is a great circle, all **longitude** lines are parts of great circles.

Given two points on the surface of the earth, the shortest distance between them (along the surface) is along a great circle route. (See diagram above.)

Group A set of numbers, letters, etc., is said to form a group under a **binary operation** ∗ if the four following properties hold.

(a) The set is **closed** under the operation ∗.
(b) The operation ∗ is **associative**.
(c) An **identity** element exists and is unique.
(d) Each element of the set has a unique **inverse**.

For example, all 2 by 2 **matrices** with non-zero **determinant** form a group under matrix multiplication.

The numbers 1, 5, 7, 11 form a group under multiplication **modulo** 12.

Hectare An **area** of 10,000 **square metres**. A square of side 100 m has an area of 1 hectare.

Helix A helix is a curve which lies on the surface of a **cylinder** or **cone** and makes a constant angle with the **axis**.

Hemisphere A hemisphere is half of a **sphere** and is formed when a sphere is cut into two, the cut passing through the sphere's centre.

Heptagon A heptagon is a seven-sided **polygon**.
   The sum of all the interior angles of a heptagon is 900°.

a regular heptagon
(all sides equal)

Hero's formula A formula for the **area** of a triangle.

$$A = \sqrt{s(s-a)(s-b)(s-c)}$$

where $s = \frac{1}{2}(a + b + c)$

Hexagon A hexagon is a **polygon** having six sides.

The diagram shows a **regular** hexagon, each of whose interior angles is equal to 120°.

Highest common factor The highest common factor (or HCF) of two or more numbers is the largest number that divides exactly into each of them. For example:

HCF of 6, 8, 12 is 2
HCF of 10, 15, 20 is 5
HCF of 20 and 45 is 5
HCF of 42 and 56 is 14

Histogram A histogram is similar to a **bar chart** except that the **frequency** of the bar is represented by its area rather than its height.

length of phone call (minutes)	Number of calls	calls/minute
0–1	10	$10 \div 1 = 10$
1–2	15	$15 \div 1 = 15$
2–5	15	$15 \div 3 = 5$
5–10	20	$20 \div 5 = 4$

Homogeneous A homogeneous **polynomial** is one whose terms are all of the same **degree**.

$x^3 + x^2y + 3xy^2 + 7y^3$ is homogeneous of degree 3
or
$2x^2 + 3xy - y^2$ is homogeneous of degree 2.

Note: the degree of the term is obtained by adding together the powers of x and y, so x^3y^4 is of degree 7.

Similarly a homogeneous **equation** may be defined. For example:

$x^3 + x^2y + 3xy^2 + 7y^3 = 0$ is homogeneous of degree 3.

Hooke's law Hooke's law states that the extension of a spring is proportional to the load put on it (provided that the spring returns to its unstretched length when the load is removed).

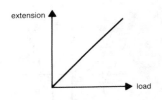

$E \propto L$ or $E = k \times L$ where k is a constant depending on the properties of the material of the spring.

Horizontal A line is said to be horizontal if it is parallel to the earth's skyline.

A liquid which is at rest has a horizontal surface.

Hour A unit of time. 1 hour = 60 minutes, and there are 24 hours in a day.

Hyperbola A hyperbola is a curve of the **conic** family. It is the **locus** of a point which moves so that the ratio of its distance from a fixed point (called the **focus**) to its distance from a fixed line (called the **directrix**) is a constant greater than 1.

The ratio:

$$\frac{PF_1}{PQ} = e > 1$$

$$F_2P - F_1P = 2a$$

The ratio e is called the **eccentricity** of the hyperbola.

A hyperbola has two foci (plural of focus). The two dotted lines in the diagram above are called the **asymptotes** of the hyperbola. The Cartesian equation of the hyperbola drawn opposite is

$$\frac{x^2}{a^2} - \frac{y^2}{b^2} = 1$$

It has a focus (a,o) and a directrix line $x = \frac{a^2}{c}$ where $c^2 = a^2 + b^2$. The asymptotes are the lines

$$\frac{y}{b} = \frac{x}{a} \quad \text{and} \quad \frac{y}{b} = \frac{-x}{a}$$

Hypocycloid A hypocycloid is the **locus** of a point P fixed on the **circumference** of a circle which rolls on the inside of a given fixed circle.

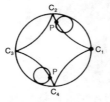

C_1, C_2, C_3, C_4 are called **cusps**. In the diagram the fixed circle has a diameter four times that of the rolling circle.

Hypotenuse The hypotenuse is the longest side of a **right-angled** triangle. The hypotenuse is always opposite the right angle.

Hypothesis A hypothesis is an assumption which is made on the basis of past observations, which is then used as a condition when proving the truth of some further proposition.

Icosahedron An icosahedron is a **polyhedron** having 20 faces. A **regular** icosahedron is made up of 20 **equilateral** triangles.

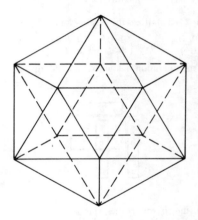

Identity An identity of a set *S* with **binary operation** * is a member *i* of the set which, when combined with any other member of the set, leaves it unchanged: $i * x = x * i = x$ for $x \in S$.

For example, for addition, 0 is the identity since $0 + 7 = 7$, $0 + -2 = -2$, $0 + 150 = 150$, etc.

101

For multiplication, 1 is the identity since $1 \times 7 = 7$, $1 \times -2 = -2$, $1 \times 19 = 19$, etc.

For **sets** under the operation of **union**, Ø, (the **empty set**) is the identity:

Ø ∪ {a, b, c, d} = {a, b, c, d}. Ø ∪ A = A (for any A).

For 2×2 **matrices** the identity for multiplication is:

$$\begin{pmatrix} 1 & 0 \\ 0 & 1 \end{pmatrix} \text{ since } \begin{pmatrix} 1 & 0 \\ 0 & 1 \end{pmatrix} \begin{pmatrix} a & b \\ c & d \end{pmatrix} = \begin{pmatrix} a & b \\ c & d \end{pmatrix}$$

In the operation below, b is the identity.

	a	b	c	d
a	d	a	b	c
b	a	b	c	d
c	b	c	d	a
d	c	d	a	b

Note: the 'b' row is the same as the top row of the table, and the 'b' column is the same as the left column of the table.

Image The result of applying a **function** to a particular member of the **domain** is called the image of that element. For example: $x \rightarrow 2x + 3$, $2 \rightarrow 7$. The number 7 is said to be the image of the number 2 which is called the object.

A

object triangle

B   C

0

B'   A'

image of triangle ABC after a 90° rotation
about the origin

C'

In geometry the term is often applied to the result of
some **transformation**.

Imaginary The imaginary part of a complex **number** $a + bi$ is b. For example, the imaginary part of $3 + 4i$ is 4.

Improper An improper fraction is one whose **numerator** is greater than its **denominator**. For example, $^{17}/_6$, $^{8}/_3$, $^{13}/_4$, etc.

An improper fraction may be changed into a **mixed number**. For example, $^{17}/_6 = 2^5/_6$, $^{13}/_4 = 3^1/_4$.

Inch A unit of length. There are 12 inches in 1 **foot** and 1 inch is just bigger than 2.5 centimetres.

Incircle In the triangle below, the angles have been **bisected**. All these bisectors meet at the same point 0, called the *incentre* of the triangle. With 0 as centre it is possible to draw a circle that just touches each of the sides of the triangle. This circle is called the incircle, or **inscribed** circle of the triangle.

Independent The equation $y = 2x + 5$ defines y as a function of x. x is said to be the independent **variable** of the function (and y is the dependent variable).

In the equation $S = 2t^2 + 3t - 5$, the independent variable is t.

Index (plural: indices) In the number 2^3, 3 is called the index or **power**.

When numbers are multiplied or divided, the rules given below apply:
$x^a \times x^b = x^{a+b}$ (add indices when multiplying)
$x^a \div x^b = x^{a-b}$ (subtract indices when dividing)
$(x^a)^b = x^{ab}$
Using these rules, negative and fractional indices may be deduced:

$$x^{-a} = \frac{1}{x^a}, \; x^{1/n} = \sqrt[n]{x}, \text{ and } x^{a/b} = \sqrt[b]{x^a} \text{ or } (\sqrt[b]{x})^a$$

also $x^\circ = 1$ for any number x

$$2^{-5} = \frac{1}{2^5} = \frac{1}{32}, \; 125^{1/3} = \sqrt[3]{125} = 5,$$

$$8^{2/3} = \sqrt[3]{8^2} = \sqrt[3]{64} = 4$$

When a number (for example, 16) is written as $16 = 2^4$, it is said to be written in index form. Similarly,

$$360 = 2 \times 2 \times 2 \times 3 \times 3 \times 5$$
$$= 2^3 \times 3^2 \times 5^1.$$

Inequality An inequality or ordering is a mathematical statement that one quantity is greater or less than another. For example:

$3 > 2$ (3 is greater than 2)
$1 < 4$ (1 is less than 4)
$x \geqslant 1$ (x is greater than or equal to 1)
$y \leqslant 2$ (y is less than or equal to 2)

Inequalities remain true if the same quantity is added to or subtracted from both sides, or if both sides are multiplied or divided by the same positive number. However multiplying or dividing by a negative number changes the sense of the inequality:

$$5 > 2 \text{ adding } 3 \quad 8 > 5$$

subtract 4 $1 > -2$

× by 3 $15 > 6$

÷ by 2 $2\tfrac{1}{2} > 1$ } all still true

but

× by −4 $-20 < -8$

÷ by −2 $-2\tfrac{1}{2} < -1$ } direction of sign must change to make the statement true

Inequation A statement involving **inequalities**. For example:

$$x^2 + 2x + 2 > 0$$

holds for any numerical value of x.

$y < 3x - 1$ is satisfied by all points below the line $y = 3x - 1$.

$y < 3x - 1$ for all points (x, y) in the shaded region.

106

Infinite   A quantity is said to be infinite if it is larger than any fixed limit. For example, the set, {1, 2, 3, 4, . . .} has an infinite number of members. But the set, {a, b, c, . . . y, z} has a finite number of members, since they can be counted (26 members).

The symbol ∞ is used to represent an infinite value, or infinity.

Inflection   A point of inflection on a curve is where the curve changes from being **concave** upwards to concave downwards (or vice versa). The point P below is said to be a **stationary point** of inflection since the **gradient** at P is zero. Q is a non-stationary inflection since the gradient is non-zero at Q.

gradient
is zero
at P

non-zero
gradient
at Q

At a point of inflection the **tangent** crosses the curve.

Inscribed   A circle is inscribed in a **polygon** if each side of the polygon is **tangent** to the circle.

The inscribed circle in a triangle has its centre at the point of **intersection** of the angle **bisectors**.

Integer An integer is a **whole number**. For example:

$$\ldots -5, -4, -3, -2, -1, 0, +1, +2, +3, +4, +5 \ldots$$

    negative integers   **positive** integers

Integral The integral of the function $f(x)$ is defined as the limit as δx approaches zero, of the sum of the areas of the rectangles under the curve (see diagram below).

The area under the curve between the values $x = a$ and $x = b$ is written as:

$$\int_a^b f(x)\, dx$$

This is called a *definite integral* and a and b are known as the *lower* and *upper* limits of the integral.

Any function whose **derivative** is $f(x)$ is called an *indefinite integral* of $f(x)$ For example, $3x^2 + 7$, $3x^2 - 14$, $3x^2 + K$ are all indefinite integrals of $6x$.

Integration Integration is the process of finding a definite or indefinite **integral**. Integration may be thought of as the inverse of **differentiation**.

Some important results are:

$\int x^n dx = \dfrac{1}{n+1}\, x^{n+1} + K$ (for n $\neq -1$)

$\int \sin x\, dx = -\cos x + K$

$\int \cos x\, dx = \sin x + K$

Intercept The intercept of a straight line on an axis is the distance from the origin to the point where the line cuts the axis. See diagram over page.

In the diagram above, for example, the x and y intercepts are -4 and 2 respectively.

Interest Interest is a charge made for borrowing money. There are two main ways of calculating interest.

Simple interest is where the interest is worked out over the whole period, just on the capital borrowed:

$$\text{Simple interest} = \frac{P \times R \times T}{100}$$

P = amount borrowed
R = rate of interest (per cent)
T = time of loan

When the interest due is added onto the amount borrowed, and then itself earns interest, it is called **compound interest**: interest + capital at compound interest of six per cent means that $P \times 1.06^n$ is owed after n years.

Interpolation Interpolation is the process of finding the value of a function at a point using two known values on either side of the point.

110

For example, using linear interpolation the predicted value of $f(c)$ using the known values $f(a)$ and $f(b)$, is shown on the diagram below.

Interquartile range The interquartile range of a **distribution** of numbers is the difference between the upper and lower **quartiles** of the distribution.

IQR = (upper quartile) − (lower quartile)

1 2 2 4 6 7 7 7 8 9 9

lower
quartile

interquartile range
is 6

upper
quartile

Intersection The intersection of two lines or curves is the set of points in common to the two.

two lines intersecting
in a single point

a line intersecting a
circle in two points

P_1

P_1 P_2

The intersection of two sets is the set of elements that they have in common.

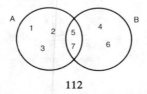

A   B

1   2   5   4

3   7   6

$A = \{1, 2, 3, 5, 7\}$, $B = \{4, 5, 6, 7\} \Rightarrow A \cap B = \{5, 7\}$
Note: the symbol $\cap$ means intersection.

Interval If x is a real number and can take all values between -2 and $+3$ inclusive, we say that x lies in the interval -2 to $+3$. This may be represented in a diagram using a number line.

The diagram above shows the 'end points' are included. Algebraically this interval is written as:

$$\{x: -2 \leqslant x \leqslant 3\} \text{ or } [-2, 3]$$

and is sometimes called a **closed** interval, since both end points are included.

An interval where the end points are not included is called an open interval:

The open interval: $\{x: -1 < x < 5\}$ or $]-1, 5[$

The diagram above shows the 'end points' are not included.

An interval may be half open and half closed:

$$\{x: -2 \leqslant x < 4\} \text{ or } [-2, 4[$$

The diagram above shows -2 included in the interval and 4 excluded.

Invariant A quantity or property is invariant under a **transformation** if it remains unchanged by the transformation. For example, the areas of plane figures remain invariant under certain transformations such as **rotations, reflections, shears, translations**.

Inverse If a set with a **binary** operation $*$ defined on it has an **identity** element i, then any element x for which there exists another element x^{-1} with $x * x^{-1} = i$ is said to have an inverse element. For example:

The inverse of $+7$ under addition is -7.
The inverse of 8 under multiplication is $\frac{1}{8}$.
The inverse of the **matrix** $\begin{pmatrix} 5 & 3 \\ 6 & 4 \end{pmatrix}$ under

multiplication is $\begin{pmatrix} 2 & -1\frac{1}{2} \\ -3 & 2\frac{1}{2} \end{pmatrix}$.

The inverse of the **function** $f(x) = \dfrac{x-1}{2}$ is $f^{-1}(x) = 2x + 1$.

The inverse of the plane **transformation** 'rotate through $+90°$ about $(0, 0)$ is 'rotate through $-90°$ about $(0, 0)$'.

Inversely Two quantities vary inversely if they are inversely **proportional** to each other.

Involute The involute of a circle is the curve described by the end of a thread as it is unwound from a fixed spool (keeping the thread taut all the time).

The distances d_1, d_2, d_3, . . . are equal to ¼, ½, ¾, etc. of the **circumference** of the circle.

Irrational number An irrational number is one that is not **rational**, that is, it cannot be expressed as a fraction, or written in exact form as a finite decimal. For example, π, e, $\sqrt{2}$, $\sqrt{3}$, $1 - \sqrt{7}$. All the irrational numbers together with all the rational numbers make the set of real numbers.

It can be shown that $\sqrt{2}$ is an irrational number as follows:

Suppose $\sqrt{2}$ is rational

i.e. $\sqrt{2} = \dfrac{a}{b}$ (where this fraction has been fully cancelled)

$\therefore 2 = \dfrac{a^2}{b^2}$

$\therefore 2b^2 = a^2$ since $2b^2$ is always even, then a must be even, e.g., $a = 2p$

$\therefore 2b^2 = (2p)^2$ (replacing a by $2p$)

$\therefore 2b^2 = 4p^2$

$\therefore b^2 = 2p^2$ since $2p^2$ is always even, then b must be even.

We have proved both a and b are even, which means that they have a common factor of 2, so the fraction a/b cancels by 2. This is clearly a contradiction, therefore the original assumption that $\sqrt{2}$ could be expressed as a fraction must have been invalid.

Isometric   Isometric graph paper is paper ruled into **equilateral** triangles rather than squares.

116

Isometry An isometry is a transformation under which all lengths are **invariant**. For example, **translations**, **rotations**, **reflections** are isometries; **shears** and **enlargements** are not.

Isometries that preserve **sense** also are called *direct* isometries, and those that change sense are called *opposite* isometries.

translation
(direct)

rotation
(direct)

reflection
(opposite)

Isomorphic Two groups are isomorphic if they have the same structure. There is a one-one **correspondence** φ between the groups such that $\varphi(a*b) = \varphi(a).\varphi(b)$ for all a and b. φ is called an *isomorphism*. For example:

(A)	0	1	2	3
0	0	1	2	3
1	1	2	3	0
2	2	3	0	1
3	3	0	1	2

(addition)
modulo 4

(B)	0°	90°	180°	270°
0°	0	90	180	270
90°	90	180	270	0
180°	180	270	0	90
270°	270	0	90	180

(combining)
rotations

Note: 0 in table (A) above, corresponds to 0° in table (B). 1 in table (A) corresponds to 90° in table (B), etc.

The mapping: $0 \to 0°$ (**identities** correspond)
$1 \to 90°$
$2 \to 180°$ (**self-inverse** members correspond)
$3 \to 270°$

from (A) to (B) is an isomorphism. Or equally well, the isomorphism could have been $0 \to 0°$, $1 \to 270°$, $2 \to 180°$, $3 \to 90°$.

Also note that each group comprises identity, one self-inverse element and an inverse pair.

(C)	a	b	c	d
a	a	b	c	d
b	b	a	d	c
c	c	d	a	b
d	d	c	b	a

(D)	1	2	3	4
1	1	2	3	4
2	2	4	1	3
3	3	1	4	2
4	4	3	2	1

(E)	1	2	3	4
1	1	2	3	4
2	2	4	3	1
4	4	3	1	2
3	3	1	2	4

(multiplication)
modulo 5

(C) is not isomorphic to (A) and (B) since every element of (C) is self-inverse. (D) is isomorphic to

118

(A) and (B) but the table may need rearranging as in (E) to make this more obvious.

The set of positive real numbers under the operation of multiplication is isomorphic to the set of real numbers under addition using the isomorphism $x \rightarrow \log x$. This is the basis for the use of the logarithm function as a calculating aid. The study of isomorphic systems is an important branch of modern algebra, as results proved about one system can be applied to the second.

Isosceles   An isosceles triangle is one that has two sides and two angles equal.

An isosceles **trapezium** is one whose two non-**parallel** sides are equal.

Each of the above figures has one line of **symmetry** (as shown in the diagrams).

119

Iterate To iterate means to repeat. So,

$$\frac{d^3y}{dx^3}$$

is an iterated differential, since y is **differentiated** three times.

Iterative An iterative process involves the repetition of a sequence of operations to improve some result. For example:

is an iterative way of finding $\sqrt[3]{10}$.

Kilogram   A unit of mass: 1 kilogram = 1000 **grams** (1 kg = 1000 g). 1 kg is approximately 2.2 lbs.

Kilometre   A unit of distance: 1 kilometre = 1000 **metres** (1 km = 1000 m). 1 km is approximately ⅝ of a **mile**.

Kite   A kite is a **quadrilateral** having two pairs of adjacent sides equal.

A kite has one line of **symmetry**. This diagonal **bisects**

the figure. The second diagonal is at right angles to the first diagonal but neither bisects the first nor the figure.

Knot   A knot is a unit of speed equivalent to one **nautical mile** per hour.

Königsberg bridge problem An historic problem in **topology** attributed to the famous Swiss mathematician Euler. It concerns the possibility of

crossing each of the seven bridges in the town of Königsberg just once and returning to a starting point. By analysing the **network** of routes Euler showed the journey was not possible.

Latin square A Latin square is a square array of numbers or letters in which each number or letter appears once in every row and column. For example:

<table>
<tr><td>1 2 3 4</td><td rowspan="4">but not</td><td>p q r s</td></tr>
<tr><td>4 3 2 1</td><td>q r s p</td></tr>
<tr><td>3 1 4 2</td><td>r q p s</td></tr>
<tr><td>2 4 1 3</td><td>s p r p</td></tr>
</table>

The combination table for a **group** must be a Latin square.

Latitude A parallel of latitude is a circle drawn on the earth's surface, whose centre is on the line joining the north and south poles. All latitude lines are parallel to each other, hence the term, 'parallel of latitude'. The latitude of any point is given by the angle ∠ A0B where 0 is the centre of the earth and A and B are points on the required latitude line and the **equator** respectively. A and B are on the same **longitude** line. All latitude lines, apart from the equator, are **small circles**.

A has latitude 60° North

Limit A **sequence** is said to tend to a limit if its terms approach a definite value, getting ever closer as more and more terms are included. Similarly the sum of a **series** may tend to a limit. For example:

$1, 1\frac{1}{2}, 1\frac{3}{4}, 1\frac{7}{8}, 1\frac{15}{16} \ldots$ limit is 2
$7.1, 7.01, 7.001, 7.0001 \ldots$ limit is 7
$4 + 2 + 1 + \frac{1}{2} + \frac{1}{4} + \frac{1}{8} + \ldots$ limit of the sum is 8
$6 + 2 + \frac{2}{3} + \frac{2}{9} + \frac{2}{27} + \ldots$ limit of the sum is 9
$a + ar + ar^2 + ar^3 + \ldots$ limit of the sum of the
geometric progression is
$a/(1 - r), (-1 < r < 1)$

Line segment A line segment is part of a straight line:

For example, AB is a line segment, being part of the line l. The points A and B do not necessarily have to be part of the line segment.

Linear A general term pertaining to systems related in some way to straight lines.

A linear relationship between two variables x and y, is one that can be represented graphically by a straight line. Equations of such relationships (linear equations) can be written in the form $y = mx + c$.

$y = 2x + 3$

The value of *m* gives the **gradient** of the line graph.
The value of *c* gives the **intercept** of the graph on the
y-axis.

Litre A litre is a measure of **volume** equal to 1000
cubic centimetres. 1 litre = 1000 cm^3. There are just
over 4.5 litres in 1 **gallon**.

Locus The path of a moving point.

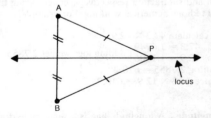

The locus of a point P, which moves so that it is
equidistant from two fixed points A and B, is the
perpendicular bisector of the line joining A and B.

Logarithm The logarithm of a number to a given **base**, is the **power** to which the base must be raised to give that number. For example:

$\log_{10} 100 = 2$ since $10^2 = 100$ (base = 10)
$\log_2 64 = 6$ since $2^6 = 64$ (base = 2)
$\log_5 0.008 = -3$ since $5^{-3} = 0.008$ (base = 5)

Logarithms to base 10 are called **common logarithms** and to base e ($e = 2.718 \ldots$) are called **natural** or **Naperian logarithms**. The natural logarithm function, usually written $\log_e x$ or $\ln x$ is an important function in the study of **calculus**.

Before the introduction of calculators, logarithms were particularly useful since they reduced multiplication and division problems into problems of addition and subtraction respectively, hence saving time and tedious numerical working. For example:

To calculate 47.3×12.9
$\left.\begin{array}{l} \log_{10} 47.3 = 1.6749 \\ \log_{10} 12.9 = 1.1106 \end{array}\right\}$ adding logs we get 2.7855
Antilog 2.7855 = 610.2
Hence $47.3 \times 12.9 \simeq 610.2$

Longitude A longitude line is a semi-circle drawn on the surface of the earth joining the north and south poles. Longitude lines are parts of **great circles**, that is, circles having the same radius as that of the earth.

Just as **latitude** is measured in degrees north or south of the **equator**, so longitude is measured in degrees east or west of Greenwich, a fixed longitude line passing through Greenwich, London. (Known as the Greenwich meridian.)

If in the diagram above, NPS represents the Greenwich line (0°) and angles P0A and P0B are 30° and 20° respectively, then all points on the line NAS are on the longitude 30°W line, and all points on line NBS are on the 20°E line.

Lower bound A lower bound of a set of numbers, is a number that is less than or equal to every member of the set. For example, $\{1/2, 1/3, 1/4, 1/5 \ldots\}$ has a lower bound of 0.

Lowest 1. The lowest common multiple (LCM) of two or more numbers is the smallest number that they will divide into exactly. For example:

$$\text{LCM of 2, 3, 4 is 12}$$
$$\text{LCM of 18, 27 is 54}$$
$$\text{LCM of 8, 16 is 16}$$
$$\text{LCM of } x, 2x, x^2 \text{ is } 2x^2$$

2. The lowest common **denominator** of a set of fractions is the denominator that is the lowest common multiple of all the denominators. For example:

lowest common denominator of $3/4$, $5/6$ and $1/3$ is 12

lowest common denominator of $\dfrac{2}{x+1}$ and $\dfrac{4}{x^2-1}$ is $x^2 - 1$

3. A fraction is said to be in its lowest terms if it has been **cancelled** as much as possible. For example:

128

$\dfrac{3}{4}, \dfrac{5}{7}, \dfrac{1}{x-1}, \dfrac{3}{x^2}$ are in their lowest terms,

but

$\dfrac{6}{9}, \dfrac{20}{25}, \dfrac{x-1}{x^2-1}, \dfrac{3x}{x^4}$

are not since they will cancel down to

$\dfrac{2}{3}, \dfrac{4}{5}, \dfrac{1}{x+1}$ and $\dfrac{3}{x^3}$ respectively.

Magic square A magic square is a square array of numbers in which every **row**, **column** and the two **diagonals** add up to give the same total. For example:

(A)

8	1	6
3	5	7
4	9	2

(total 15)

(B)

27	1	17	7
16	8	26	2
5	15	3	29
4	28	6	14

(total 52)

Example (B) above is rather special since in addition each block of four corners adds up to 52, the block of four in the centre adds up to 52 and the shorter diagonals $(16 + 1 + 6 + 29)$ and $(5 + 8 + 17 + 2)$ add up to 52. The four corners add up to 52 and the middle two numbers of the top and bottom rows add up to 52. Also the middle two numbers of the left and right columns add up to 52!

Magnitude The magnitude of a **vector** is the length of the vector, when represented in line segment form.

130

By **Pythagoras' Theorem** $3^2 + 4^2 = 5^2$. So the magnitude is 5.

Major **1.** The longer of the two **axes** of symmetry of an **ellipse** is called the major axis. The other is called the **minor** axis. For an ellipse with equation:

$$\frac{x^2}{a^2} + \frac{y^2}{b^2} = 1 \ (a > b)$$

The major axis has length $2a$.

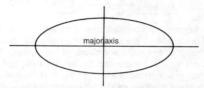

2. The shaded part of the diagram shows a major **sector** of the circle. The arc ACB is called a major **arc** of the circle.

Mapping   A mapping is a **function**. If the members of the set {8, 6, 4, 2} are each halved, a new set {4, 3, 2, 1} is formed. Halving transforms members of one set into members of another.

The diagram above illustrates what happens to the numbers 8, 6, 4, 2. We say that the members of one set are mapped onto the members of the other. The numbers 4, 3, 2, 1 are called the **images** of 8, 6, 4, 2.

A mapping or function is a special type of relation in which every member of the set has one image.

A mapping diagram is a diagram to illustrate a mapping.

$$x \to x + 3$$

132

Matrix A matrix is a rectangular array of numbers. For example:

$$A = \begin{pmatrix} 3 & 5 \\ 2 & 4 \end{pmatrix} \qquad B = \begin{pmatrix} 6 & 3 & 1 \\ 5 & 2 & 7 \end{pmatrix}$$

$$C = \begin{pmatrix} 8 & 1 \\ 6 & 2 \\ 5 & 3 \end{pmatrix} \qquad D = \begin{pmatrix} 10 & 5 \\ 4 & 2 \end{pmatrix}$$

Matrix A has two **rows** and two **columns**. Matrix B has two rows and three columns.

Matrices of the same order (i.e., with the same number of rows and columns) can be added, by adding corresponding elements. For example:

$$A + D = \begin{pmatrix} 3+10, & 5+5 \\ 2+4, & 4+2 \end{pmatrix} = \begin{pmatrix} 13 & 10 \\ 6 & 6 \end{pmatrix}$$

Matrices A and B are compatible for multiplication because A has as many columns as B has rows. Multiplication involves the combining of the rows of A with the columns of B:

$$A \times B =$$
$$\begin{pmatrix} 3\times6+5\times5, & 3\times3+5\times2, & 3\times1+5\times7 \\ 2\times6+4\times5, & 2\times3+4\times2, & 2\times1+4\times7 \end{pmatrix}$$

$$= \begin{pmatrix} 43 & 19 & 38 \\ 32 & 14 & 30 \end{pmatrix}$$

Square matrices with non-zero **determinants** have multiplicative **inverses**:

The inverse of $\begin{pmatrix} a & b \\ c & d \end{pmatrix} = \dfrac{1}{ad-bc} \begin{pmatrix} d & -b \\ -c & a \end{pmatrix}$

For example: $A^{-1} = \begin{pmatrix} 2 & -2\frac{1}{2} \\ -1 & 1\frac{1}{2} \end{pmatrix}$

Matrices are a very powerful tool in the study of the solutions of **linear** equations.

Maximum

The graph shown above is said to have a maximum point at the point P.

The **tangent** drawn to the curve at the point P would have zero **gradient**. Just to the left of P, the tangent would have a positive gradient and just to the right it would be negative.

Mean The arithmetic mean of a set of numbers is the sum of all the numbers divided by the number of figures in the set. (Often called the 'average'). For example, the mean of 2, 6, 8, 9, 12 is:

$$\frac{2 + 6 + 8 + 9 + 12}{5} = \frac{37}{5} = 7 \cdot 4.$$

score on a dice	1	2	3	4	5	6	(total 20
number of throws	5	3	4	2	3	3	throws)

The mean score is:

$$\frac{(1 \times 5) + (2 \times 3) + (3 \times 4) + (4 \times 2) + (5 \times 3) + (6 \times 3)}{20}$$

$$= \frac{64}{20} = 3 \cdot 2.$$

Mean deviation The mean deviation (or strictly speaking — the mean **absolute** deviation from the arithmetic **mean**) of a list of numbers is defined as:

$$\frac{\text{sum of all deviations from the mean}}{\text{number of figures in the list}}$$

For example, for 7, 3, 10, 4 the mean is 24/4 = 6, and hence the deviations from the mean are 1, 3, 4, 2. Therefore the mean deviation is:

$$\frac{1 + 3 + 4 + 2}{4} = \frac{10}{4} = 2\frac{1}{2}.$$

Median The median of a set of numbers is the value of the middle number, when they are arranged in ascending order. Examples:

For 1, 2, 4, 7, 9 the median is 4.
2, 5, 8, 3, 1, 7, 6 becomes 1, 2, 3, 5, 6, 7, 8 and the median is 5.

If there is no middle number, the average of the two middle numbers is taken. For example:

For 1, 5, 7, 8, 9, 10 the median is $\frac{7+8}{2} = 7\frac{1}{2}$.

The median of a **frequency distribution** is found from the **cumulative frequency** graph or **ogive**.

Member A number, letter, symbol, etc., that belongs to a **set** is said to be a member of the set. For example:

2 is a member of the set of even numbers
a is a member of the set of vowels

but 4 is not a member of the set of odd numbers.

The mathematical symbols used for 'is a member of' and 'is not a member of' are $\in$ and $\notin$ respectively. For example:

$2 \in \{$prime numbers$\}$
$s \in \{$letters of the alphabet$\}$
$p \notin \{$vowels$\}$
$\alpha \notin \{\beta, \gamma, \pi, \varrho\}$

Mensuration The measuring of geometrical quantities, for example, lengths, areas and volumes.

Meridian A meridian is a **great circle** drawn on the earth's surface which passes through the north and south poles. For example, all **longitude lines** may be referred to as meridians.

Metre A metre is a unit of length (just over 39 **inches**). 1 metre = 100 **centimetres** (1 m = 100 cm).

Metric A system of units of measurement in which the fundamental units of length, mass, etc., are divided and compounded by factors of ten. For example, 1 **kilogram** = 1000 **grams**, 1 **metre** = 100 centimetres.
  The prefixes kilo-, hecto-, deca-, deci-, centi-, milli-, denote multiples of 10^3, 10^2, 10, 1/10, 1/100, 1/1000.

Mile A unit of length. 1 mile = 5280 **feet** or 1760 **yards**. 1 mile is approximately 1.6 **kilometres**.

Millimetre A unit of length. There are 10 millimetres in 1 **centimetre**. 1 millimetre equals 0.1 cm, 10 mm = 1 cm.

Million One thousand thousand. One million equals 1,000,000 = 10^6.

Minimum The graph shown is said to have a minimum point at the point P.

The **tangent** drawn to the curve at this point would have zero **gradient**. Just to the right of P the gradient is positive and just to the left, it is negative.

Minor 1. The shorter of the two **axes** of symmetry of an ellipse is called the minor axis. The other is called the **major** axis. For an ellipse with equation:

$$\frac{x^2}{a^2} + \frac{y^2}{b^2} = 1 \ (a > b)$$

the minor axis has length 2b.

2. The shaded part of the diagram below, shows a minor **sector** of the circle. The **arc ACB** is called a minor arc of the circle.

Minute **1.** A unit of time. There are 60 seconds in 1 minute, and 60 minutes in 1 **hour**.

2. A unit of angular measure. There are 60 minutes in 1 **degree** (60′ = 1°).

Mixed number A mixed number is the sum of a whole number and a fraction: $2\frac{1}{2}$, $3\frac{2}{5}$, $-6\frac{7}{8}$ are all mixed numbers.

A mixed number can be changed into an **improper fraction** as follows:

$$2^{5}/_{7} = \frac{(2 \times 7) + 5}{7} = \frac{19}{7} \text{ or } 3^{9}/_{10} = \frac{(3 \times 10) + 9}{10} = \frac{39}{10}$$

Mode The mode of a set of numbers is the number that occurs most often in the set. For example:

1, 2, 3, 3, 4, 6, 9: mode is 3
3, 4, 4, 4, 7, 7, 8: mode is 4
2, 2, 3, 5, 6, 9, 9: this set has two modes, 2 and 9, and is said to be **bimodal**.

score on die	1	2	3	4	5	6
number of throws	5	6	2	4	3	5

mode is 2, since 2 was thrown most often (6 times)

In a grouped **frequency** distribution the group that contains most members is called the modal group or modal class. For example:

height of children (cm)	50—54	55—59	60—64	65—69
number of children	7	2	4	3

The modal group is 50—54 cm.

Modulo arithmetic In arithmetic modulo n, all numbers are represented by their remainder when divided by n. In modulo 8, $6 + 5 = 3$, $4 \times 3 = 4$, etc.

This type of arithmetic can be modelled by moving round a clockface.

$6 + 5 \equiv$ start at 6, then move on 5 places, to finish at 3.

In arithmetic modulo p, where p is **prime**, equations of the form $ax + b = c$ have unique solutions.

Modulus **1.** The modulus or **absolute value** of a real number x, denoted by $|x|$ is the positive value of x, regardless of its sign. For example: $|3.5| = 3.5, |-7| = 7$.

2. The modulus of a **complex number** is its distance from the **origin** when represented on the **Argand diagram**.

The modulus of the complex number $a + bi$, denoted by $|a + bi|$, is $\sqrt{a^2 + b^2}$.

Multiple The number x is a multiple of the number y if y divides x exactly. For example, 5, 10, 15, 20 ... are all multiples of 5.

Multiplication One of the fundamental operations of arithmetic. Multiplication is associated with repeated addition. For example,
$5 \times 3 = 5 + 5 + 5 = 15$.

Analogous operations on abstract mathematical systems are sometimes known as multiplication. For example:

matrix multiplication $\begin{pmatrix} 3 & 1 \\ 4 & 2 \end{pmatrix} \times \begin{pmatrix} 1 & 2 \\ 3 & 4 \end{pmatrix}$

$$= \begin{pmatrix} 6 & 10 \\ 10 & 16 \end{pmatrix}$$

Natural The set of **positive whole numbers** (counting numbers) are called the natural numbers.

The set of natural numbers {1, 2, 3, 4, . . .} is often denoted by ℕ.

Natural **logarithms** are logarithms to the base of **e**.

Nautical mile A nautical mile (or sea mile) is a distance of 6080 feet, and is equivalent to one **minute** of arc measured along a **great circle** on the earth's surface. Hence 60 nm of great circle **subtends** an angle of 1° at the centre of the earth.

Negative A negative number is a number whose value is less than 0. For example, −2.5, −724, −0.176, −¹/₁₀ are all negative, 0, 3.5, 176, 0.001 are not negative.

Net A surface which can be folded into a solid.

Each of the shapes above is said to form a net for a **cube**, that is, if they were cut out, could be folded up to form a cube.

net of a square-based **pyramid**   net of a **tetrahedron**

Network A system of points (called **nodes**) linked together by **arcs**. A network divides the plane into a number of **regions**. The numbers of nodes, arcs and regions are related by **Euler's formula**:

$$\text{nodes} + \text{regions} = \text{arcs} + 2$$

Newton A unit of force named after the famous English mathematician. A resultant force of 1 Newton acting on a body of mass 1 kg produces an **acceleration** of 1 metre per second per second.

Newton's method A step-by-step, **iterative** method of finding the **roots** of an equation of the form: $f(x) = 0$.

If p_1 is an approximation to the root, then p_2, the **intercept** of the **tangent** to f at $x = p_1$ with the x-axis, is a better approximation.

Node A node is a point on a **network** to which one or more **arcs** lead.

Nonagon A nonagon is a nine-sided **polygon**. A **regular** nonagon has all its sides equal, and each of its interior angles measures 140°.

Normal The normal to a curve at any point is the line **perpendicular** to the **tangent** at that point.

A line (or **vector**) is said to be normal to a plane if it is perpendicular to all lines belonging to the plane. In the above figure, l and m are lines belonging to the plane. AB is perpendicular to l and m and hence the plane.

145

Notation Symbolism used in mathematics. Symbols representing quantities, operations, relations, etc., together with the conventions regarding their use. For example:

The notation 5! means $5 \times 4 \times 3 \times 2 \times 1$.

The notation $\sum_{1}^{4} i$ means $1 + 2 + 3 + 4$.

Nought The **numeral** 0 or **zero**.

Null The null set is the **empty set** and is denoted by $\varnothing$. It is a set with no **members**, for example, the set of real numbers whose **square** is negative is the null set.

Numeral Numerals are symbols used to denote numbers. For example:

Arabic numerals 0, 1, 2, 3, 4, 5, 6, 7, 8, 9
Roman numerals I, V, X, L, C, D, M

Numerator The top part of a **fraction**. For example, for $^{17}/_4$ the numerator is 17, for $^6/_{13}$ the numerator is 6.

Obtuse   An obtuse angle is greater than 90° but less than 180°.

this is an obtuse angle

Octagon   An octagon is a **polygon** having eight sides.
   A **regular** octagon has all its sides equal and all its interior angles are 135°.

Octahedron   A **polyhedron** having eight faces.
   A **rectangular** octahedron is made from eight **equilateral** triangles.

Odd   An odd number cannot be divided exactly by 2. For example, 7, 19, −107 are odd numbers.
   If n is a whole number then $2n + 1$ is always odd.

Ogive An ogive is another name for a **cumulative frequency** curve.

Ogives are often shaped as in the diagram below.

Operation An operation is a way of combining together members of a set.

Binary operations combine two members of a set to produce a third member as a result.

The study of abstract operations and their properties forms an important branch of modern algebra.

Order **1.** The order of a **matrix** is the number of **rows** and **columns** of the matrix.

$A = \begin{pmatrix} 3 & 1 & 6 \\ 2 & 5 & 8 \end{pmatrix}$ Matrix A has order 2 × 3. This means it has two rows and three columns.

2. The order of a **node** in a **network** is the number of **arcs** that lead to that node.

148

3. A figure which maps to itself by **reflections** about *n* lines has line **symmetry** of order *n*.

A figure which maps to itself in *n* ways by rotations about some centre 0 has rotational symmetry of order *n* about 0.

rotational
symmetry of
order 3

A square has line symmetry of order 4

4. A **group** with *n* elements is said to be a group of order *n*.

Ordered pair   A pair of numbers whose values and order are **significant** is termed an ordered pair. Used in particular to denote a pair of **Cartesian coordinates** specifying a point in a plane.

the ordered pairs (1, 4) and (4, 1)
specify different points

Ordered pairs such as (H, T), (H, H) etc., may also be used to specify the results of trials, for example, tossing two coins.

Ordinate The **y-coordinate**, or distance from the **horizontal** axis, of a point referred to a system of **Cartesian coordinates**.

the ordinate of P is 2
the ordinate of Q is −3

150

Origin The origin is the point where the x- and y-axes cross. It has **coordinates** $(0, 0))$ and the coordinates of all other points are measured relative to the origin.

Orthocentre The orthocentre of a triangle is the point where the **altitudes** meet.

orthocentre

Ounce A unit of mass. There are 16 ounces in 1 pound (16 oz = 1 lb) and just over 28 **grams** in 1 ounce.

Parabola The **locus** of a point which moves so that it is equidistant from a fixed point (called the **focus**) and a fixed line (the **directrix**) is called a parabola. It is a curve of the **conic** family.

The parabola $y^2 = 4ax$ has focus at the point $(a, 0)$ and directrix the line $x = -a$.

Any equation of the form $y = ax^2 + bx + c$ or $y^2 = 4ax$ will give a parabolic shape. The path of a **projectile** is approximately parabolic.

Parallel Lines in a plane that never meet no matter how far they are extended are called parallel. Parallel lines are always the same distance apart.

A pair of railway lines are parallel.

152

Parallelepiped A **polyhedron** whose faces are all **parallelograms** is called a parallelepiped.

Parallelogram A **quadrilateral** with its opposite sides equal (and **parallel**).

$$AB = DC \text{ and } AB \parallel DC$$
$$AD = BC \text{ and } AD \parallel BC$$

All parallelograms have the following properties:

(a) Diagonals **bisect** each other, and the whole shape
(b) Opposite angles are equal
(c) Rotational **symmetry** of order 2.

153

Parameter In the equation $y = mx + c$, the values m and c are called parameters and specify the characteristics of the straight line represented by the equation. (m represents the **gradient**, and c the **intercept** on the y-axis.

The parametric equation of the **parabola** $y^2 = 4x$ is $x = t^2$, $y = 2t$, each value of the parameter t gives a point on the curve.

Pascal's triangle Pascal's triangle is a pattern of numbers:

$$
\begin{array}{ccccccccccccc}
 & & & & & 1 & & & & & \\
 & & & & 1 & & 1 & & & & \\
 & & & 1 & & 2 & & 1 & & & \\
 & & 1 & & 3 & & 3 & & 1 & & \\
 & 1 & & 4 & & 6 & & 4 & & 1 & \\
1 & & 5 & & 10 & & 10 & & 5 & & 1
\end{array}
$$

Each number is the sum of the two numbers directly above it. The numbers in each row of the triangle are the **binomial coefficients** which occur in the expansion of $(x + y)^n$ for various values of n.

Penny A unit of currency, one hundred pennies (pence) = one pound (100p = £1).

Pentagon A five-sided **polygon**. A **regular** pentagon has all its sides equal and each of its interior angles is 108°. See diagram on following page.

Percentage A method of relating a fraction of a given quantity to the whole in parts per hundred. For example:

30% of something is thirty parts per hundred.

Hence $30\% \equiv \dfrac{30}{100}$ (note % means 'per cent')

Percentage changes in a quantity are calculated as follows:

If original value $= A$

new value $= B$

$$\text{per cent change} = \frac{|A - B|}{A} \times 100$$

Percentile The **range** of a frequency **distribution** is divided into 100 parts by percentiles. 15 per cent of the data lies below the fifteenth percentile, 40 per cent lies below the fortieth percentile, etc.

The **median** value of a distribution occurs at the fiftieth percentile.

Perfect A perfect number is one that is equal to the sum of its **factors** (excluding the number itself). For example:

$$6 = 1 + 2 + 3 \qquad 28 = 1 + 2 + 4 + 7 + 14$$

The third perfect number is 496.

Perimeter The perimeter of a figure is the distance measured round the **boundary** of the figure.

the perimeter
of this triangle
is 3 + 4 + 5 = 12 units

the perimeter of
this shape is 20 units
(2+2+4+2+6+4)

The perimeter of a circle is also known as the **circumference**.

Period The graph of $y = \sin x$ repeats itself every 360°. This value 360° is said to be the period of the function and $y = \sin x$ is said to be a periodic function.

$y = \sin x$

$y = \cos x$ also has period 360°

$y = \tan x$ has period 180°

$y = \sin 3x$ has period 120°

$y = \cos 24x$ has period 15°

Permutation A permutation is an ordered arrangement of a set of numbers.

For example, all possible permutations of the numbers 1, 2, 3 are 1, 2, 3, 12, 13, 23, 21, 31, 32, 123, 132, 231, 213, 312 and 321.

There are $n!$ (**factorial** n) permutations of n numbers taken all at a time. For example:

1 number has 1 permutation
2 numbers have 2 permutations
3 numbers have 6 permutations
4 numbers have 24 permutations

There are $n!/(n - r)!$ permutations of n numbers taken r at a time.

Perpendicular Two straight lines are said to be perpendicular if they meet at **right angles**.

Two planes may also be perpendicular. A line which is perpendicular to a plane is said to be **normal** to the plane.

Pi The symbol pi (π) is used to denote the ratio of the **circumference** of a circle to its **diameter**.

$$\pi = \frac{C}{D}$$

π is an **irrational** number: $\pi = 3.1415926535\ldots$ We commonly use 3.14 or 22/7 as an (approximate) value for π.

π is used in calculating lengths, areas and volumes of circular figures and solids. For example:

Area of a circle of radius R is πR^2

Volume of a **cylinder** is $\pi R^2 h$

Volume of a **sphere** is $\frac{4}{3} \times \pi R^3$

Pictogram A pictogram is a way of representing information (usually statistical) in the form of a picture.

pictogram showing
the vehicles passing
a checkpoint in one
minute

cars   (5)

buses   (2)

lorries   (3)

cycles   (2)

Pie chart A pie chart or circular diagram is another way of representing statistical information. The circle is divided into **sectors** whose areas represent the number in the set.

For example, for the information in the diagram on previous page, the angles would be:

$$\text{Car} \quad \frac{5}{12} \times 360° = 150°$$

$$\left.\begin{array}{l}\text{Bus} \\ \text{Cycle}\end{array}\right\} \frac{2}{12} \times 360° = 60° \text{ each}$$

$$\text{Lorry} \quad \frac{3}{12} \times 360° = 90°$$

Pint A measure of volume. There are 8 pints in 1 **gallon** and approximately 1.76 pints in 1 **litre**.

Plan The plan of a shape is the view of the shape when looking vertically downwards onto it.

The plan view of a cylinder is a circle.

cylinder   plan

prism

plan

A map gives a plan view of a portion of country.

Plane A plane is a flat surface.
In **Cartesian coordinates** the equation of a plane is of the form $ax + by + cz = d$.

Point Points are often described by their **coordinates**. A point has position but no real size.

Polar coordinates Polar coordinates are a system of specifying the position of points by their distance r from a fixed point, and angle θ measured from a fixed line.
Polar coordinates are of the form (r, θ) as opposed to (x, y) of **Cartesian coordinates**.

P is $(5, 30°)$

Q is $(3, 90°)$

R is $(4, 320°)$ or $(4, -40°)$

Polygon A polygon is a plane shape having three or more sides.

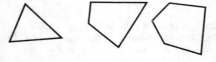

Name of polygon	Number of sides	Sum of Interior angles
Triangle	3	180°
Quadrilateral	4	360°
Pentagon	5	540°
Hexagon	6	720°
Heptagon	7	900°
Octagon	8	1080°
Decagon	10	1440°
Duodecagon	12	1800°
Icosogon	20	3240°

162

In general a polygon having n sides will have n interior angles that sum to $(n-2) \times 180°$.

Regular polygons have all their sides and all their angles equal.

Polyhedron A solid shape each of whose **faces** is a **polygon**.

There are only five **regular** polyhedra: **tetrahedron**, **cube**, **octahedron**, **dodecahedron**, **icosahedron**.

Polynomial An algebraic expression containing only positive powers of one or more **variables** $x, y, \ldots$ For example:

$3x^2 + 5x + 1$ is a **quadratic** polynomial
$y^3 + 7y + 2$ is a **cubic** polynomial
$2x^2y^3 + 3xy + 1$ is a **degree** 5 polynomial

In the polynomial $5x^4 + 3x^2 + 7x - 6$, the number 5 (which multiplies x^4) is called the **coefficient** of x^4.

Population A statistical term referring to the set of items for which a certain characteristic is being measured. Populations may be finite or infinite.

Positive A positive number is one whose value is greater than 0. For example:

735, $3\frac{1}{4}$, 0.1 are all positive

but

0, −2, −3.5 are not positive

Pound 1. A unit of currency. £1 equals 100 pence.

2. A unit of weight. One pound equals 16 **ounces** (1 lb = 16 oz), 14 pounds equals 1 stone. There are approximately 2.2 pounds in 1 kilogram (2.2 lb ≈ 1 kg).

Power For example 2 to the power 4 (written 2^4) = $2 \times 2 \times 2 \times 2 = 16$, 3 to the power 2 (written 3^2) = $3 \times 3 = 9$.

Any number to the power 2 is said to be 'squared', any number to the power 3 is said to be 'cubed'.

Prime A prime number is one that has exactly two **factors**, 1 and the number itself. There are an infinite number of prime numbers. For example, 2, 3, 5, 7, 11, 13, 17, 19, etc.

Note: 2 is the only even prime number.

Prism A prism is a **polyhedron** having the same **cross section** throughout its length.

a triangular prism

164

The volume of a prism is found by multiplying the cross sectional area by the length of the solid.

Probability Probability is a measure of how likely an event is. Its value lies between 0 (impossible event) and 1 (certain event). For example:

Probability of the sun rising in the east = 1.
Probability that Sunday is the day after Monday = 0.
Probability of throwing a head with a coin = 0.5.

In situations where several equally likely outcomes are possible, the probability of a particular event can be measured by:

$$\frac{\text{number of events favourable to the outcome}}{\text{total number of possible events}}$$

Product The product of two or more numbers is the result of **multiplying** them together. For example:

Product of 2, 3, 4 is $2 \times 3 \times 4 = 24$.
Product of 6 and 11 is $6 \times 11 = 66$.

The product of the matrices

$$\begin{pmatrix} 2 & 4 \\ 4 & 1 \end{pmatrix} \text{ and } \begin{pmatrix} 3 & 5 \\ 1 & 2 \end{pmatrix} \text{ is } \begin{pmatrix} 9 & 16 \\ 13 & 22 \end{pmatrix}$$

Progression A **sequence** of numbers each of which is related to the previous one by adding or multiplying by a fixed number. For example:

2, 5, 8, 11 is an **arithmetic** progression (add 3 to get the next term)

2, 6, 18, 54 is a **geometric** progression (multiply by 3 to get the next term)

Projectile A particle thrown into the air is known as a projectile. The path of a projectile is roughly **parabolic**.

Projection If a light was shone vertically downwards onto the horizontal plane PQRS, the line AB would cast its shadow along the line CD. CD is said to be the projection of AB onto the plane.

Proof The logical argument used to establish the truth of a statement.

Proper A proper **fraction** is one whose **numerator** is less than its **denominator**. For example, $\frac{3}{4}$ is a proper fraction but $\frac{7}{3}$ is not.

A proper **subset** A of a **set** B is a subset which does not contain all the elements of B. That is, $A \cap B = A$ but $A \cap B \neq B$. For example:

$\{1, 2, 3\}$ is a proper subset of $\{1, 2, 3, 4, 5, 6\}$ but $\{1, 2, 3, 4, 5, 6\}$ is not a proper subset of $\{1, 2, 3, 4, 5, 6\}$.

Proportion Two sets of numbers are said to be in proportion when the **ratio** between corresponding members of the two sets is constant. For example:

$\{1, 2, 5, 8, 10\}$ and $\{2, 4, 10, 16, 20\}$ are in proportion, since $1 : 2 = 2 : 4 = 5 : 10 = 8 : 16 = 10 : 20$. (That is, each member of set two is twice the corresponding member of set one.)

Two sets are inversely proportional when the members of one set are proportional to the **reciprocals** of the members of the other set. For example:

$\{1, 2, 3, 4, 6\}$ is inversely proportional to $\{12, 6, 4, 3, 2\}$

In this case the product of the corresponding elements is constant, i.e.,
$1 \times 12 = 2 \times 6 = 3 \times 4 = 4 \times 3 = 6 \times 2$.

The **circumference** of a circle is proportional to its **diameter** ($C \infty D$). The constant of proportionality is $\pi (C = \pi D)$.

Protractor A device used for measuring **angles**.

this angle measures 149°

Pyramid A pyramid is a **polyhedron** with a **polygon** for its base, the other faces being triangles with a common **vertex**.

square-based pyramid

triangular pyramid

hexagonal pyramid

The volume of a pyramid is given by:

$V = \frac{1}{3}$ (area of base) × (perpendicular height)

$V = \frac{1}{3} Ah$

A **cone** is similar to a pyramid and the formula for its volume resembles that for a pyramid:

$$V = \tfrac{1}{3} \pi r^2 h.$$

Pythagoras' Theorem This states that in any **right-angled** triangle, the area of the square on the **hypotenuse** is equal to the sum of the areas of the squares on the other sides.

A = B + C   or $z^2 = x^2 + y^2$

For example, the following triples of numbers all correspond to the lengths of sides in right-angled triangles:

$$3, 4, 5 \ (3^2 + 4^2 = 9 + 16 = 25 = 5^2)$$
$$6, 8, 10$$
$$5, 12, 13$$
$$7, 24, 25$$
$$1, 1, \sqrt{2}$$
$$1, 2, \sqrt{5}$$
$$8, 15, 17$$
$$20, 21, 29, \text{ etc.}$$

Pythagoras' Theorem is frequently used to find unknown lengths in geometrical configurations.

Quadrant 1. A quarter of a circle is called a quadrant.

2. One of the four parts that the plane is divided into by the x- and y-axes:

	y-axis	
second quadrant		first quadrant
		x-axis
third quadrant		fourth quadrant

Quadratic A quadratic **polynomial** is one of the second **degree**. For example, $3x^2 + 5x - 11$.

An equation that can be written in the form $ax^2 + bx + c = 0$ with $a \neq 0$ is called a quadratic equation.

Such equations may have two distinct, two coincident, or 0 real solutions depending upon the value of the **discriminant** of the equation.

The solutions of a general quadratic equation $ax^2 + bx + c = 0$ can be found by using the formula:

$$x = \frac{-b \pm \sqrt{b^2 - 4ac}}{2a}$$

The graph of quadratic function $y = ax^2 + bx + c$ is **parabola**-shaped.

Quadrilateral A quadrilateral is a **polygon** having four sides. **Square, rectangle, rhombus, parallelogram, kite, trapezium** are all special kinds of quadrilaterals.

examples of
quadrilaterals

Quarter The name given to one fourth part of a shape or quantity.

one quarter, ¼,
of this circle
has been shaded

three-quarters, ¾,
of this shape
has been shaded

One quarter of 12 is 3, since $12 \div 4 = 3$ or $\frac{1}{4} \times 12 = 3$.

Quartic A quartic **polynomial** is a polynomial containing powers of x up to x^4. For example, $x^4 + 2x^2 - 7x + 1$. $x^4 + 7x^3 - 2x + 3 = 0$ is a quartic equation.

Quartile A statistical measure used in connection with **cumulative frequency**. The first or lower quartile of a set of **data** is the value below which one quarter of the data lies. The second quartile (more commonly known as the **median**) is the value below which one half of the data lies, and the third or upper quartile is the value below which three-quarters of the data lies. They correspond to the 25th, 50th and 75th **percentiles**.

In a list of n numbers the lower quartile is the $\frac{1}{4}(n+1)$th number, the median is the $\frac{1}{2}(n+1)$th, and the upper quartile is the $\frac{3}{4}(n+1)$th. For example:

$$1, 2, 2, 5, 6, 7, 7, 7, 8, 9, 10$$

$$\uparrow \qquad \uparrow \qquad \uparrow$$

lower   median   upper
quartile   quartile

Lower quartile = $\frac{1}{4}(11+1)$th number = third value = 2
Median = $\frac{1}{2}(11+1)$th number = sixth value = 7
Upper quartile = $\frac{3}{4}(11+1)$th number = ninth value = 8

The **interquartile range** is 6.

Quintic A quintic **polynomial** is a polynomial containing powers of x up to x^5. For example, $x^5 + 3x^4 - 2x^2 + 7$. $x^5 + 3x^4 + 2x^3 + 6 = 0$ is a quintic equation.

Quotient The quotient is the result obtained when a **division** is performed. Examples:

$$21 \overline{)625} \quad \frac{29(r16)}{}$$ The quotient is 29 and **remainder** 16.

$$x+1 \sqrt{\begin{array}{l} x+4 \\ \overline{x^2 + 5x + 4} \end{array}}$$ The quotient is $x + 4$
$$\underline{x^2 + x} \qquad\qquad \text{with no remainder.}$$
$$\quad 4x + 4$$
$$\quad \underline{4x + 4}$$
$$\qquad\qquad 0$$

Radian The angle **subtended** at the centre of a circle by a **minor arc** of length equal to the **radius** of the circle is called a radian.

angle subtended is 1 radian

One radian $\simeq 57°$ and in a full circle there are 2π or 6.28 (approx.) radians. One **degree** equals $\dfrac{\pi}{180}$ radians.

Radius The radius of a circle is the distance from the centre of the circle to any point on the **circumference**.

Random A **sample** taken from a **population** is said to be random if every member of the population has an equal chance of being chosen.

A random number is a number in which each **digit** is chosen from the set of values 0, 1, 2, 3, 4 . . . 9, where each value has the same chance of being chosen.

Range 1. A statistical term referring to the difference between the smallest and largest members of a set of numbers. For example, for 2, 3, 4, 7, 9, 10, 12, 15, the range is $15 - 2 = 13$.

2. The range of a **function** is the set of **images** of the members of the **domain** of the function. For example: for the function $x \rightarrow 3x + 1$ with domain $\{1, 2, 3, 4\}$, the range is $\{4, 7, 10, 13\}$.

Rank When a set of numbers or quantities are arranged in ascending order, the position of any element in the list is called its rank. For example:

For the numbers	4	8	5	6	2	6	0	12
Rank order is	0	2	4	5	6	6	8	12
	↓	↓	↓	↓	↓	↓	↓	↓
Rank	1	2	3	4	5½	5½	7	8

Ratio A method of comparing two quantities measured in similar units by considering the **quotient** of the two quantities. For example:

The ratio of £2 to 50p is written: $200:50 = 4:1$.
Note: ratios are simplified similarly to **fractions**.

Rational number A rational number is any number that can be expressed in the form of a **fraction**, i.e., in the form a/b where a and b are whole numbers, and $b \neq 0$. Examples:

$$2\frac{1}{2} = \frac{5}{2} \qquad -7 = -\frac{7}{1} \qquad \sqrt{0.18} = 0.9 = \frac{9}{10}$$

The symbol for the set of all rational numbers is Q. Rational numbers can always be written as **terminating** or **recurring** decimals.

Numbers that cannot be written as a fraction are called **irrational** numbers.

Rationalize To rationalize an algebraic expression is to remove operations of the form $\sqrt{\ }$, $\sqrt[3]{\ }$, etc, without changing the value of the expression. Examples:

$\sqrt{x-2} = x$ rationalizes into $x - 2 = x^2$
or $x^2 - x + 2 = 0$

$\sqrt[3]{x^2 + 1} = 2$ rationalizes into $x^2 + 1 = 8$
or $x^2 - 7 = 0$

In the example below the **denominator** of the fraction has been rationalized:

$$\frac{1}{\sqrt{x} + y} = \frac{\sqrt{x} - y}{x - y^2}$$

To obtain this result the **numerator** and denominator of the fraction are both multiplied by $\sqrt{x} - y$.

Ray A ray is a straight line extending from a point, called the origin of the ray. Another name for a ray is a *half-line*.

The diagram above shows three rays all with 0 as common origin.

Real numbers The set of real numbers is the **union** of the sets of **rational** and **irrational** numbers.

To each point on the continuous real number line there corresponds a real number.

$$-3 \quad -2 \quad -1 \quad 0 \quad 1 \quad 2 \quad 3 \quad 4$$

$$-1.5 \quad 0.3 \quad \sqrt{2} \quad e \quad \pi$$

are all real numbers

Reciprocal The reciprocal of a non-zero number x is the number $1/x$. For example, the reciprocals of 5, $\frac{3}{4}$ and 0.4 are $\frac{1}{5}$, $1/\frac{3}{4} = \frac{4}{3}$, $1/0.4$, respectively.

The product of any number and its reciprocal is equal to 1.

Rectangle A rectangle is a **quadrilateral**, all of whose angles are equal to 90°. Opposite pairs of sides are of equal length. A rectangle has two lines of **symmetry** (shown in the diagram below) and rotational symmetry of order 2. The **diagonals** of a rectangle **bisect** each other and the figure.

Rectangle number A rectangle number is one having more than two **factors**. These numbers can be represented by rectangular configurations of dots.

Examples:

$$12 = 2 \times 6 \quad \text{or} \quad 3 \times 4$$

```
. . . . . .          . . . .
. . . . . .          . . . .
                     . . . .
```

$$20 = 2 \times 10 \quad\quad\quad \text{or} \quad\quad 4 \times 5$$

```
. . . . . . . . . .          . . . . .
. . . . . . . . . .          . . . . .
                             . . . . .
                             . . . . .
```

The set of rectangle numbers is: {4, 6, 8, 9, 10, 12, 14, 15, 16 . . .}. The set of **prime numbers** is: {2, 3, 5, 7, 11 . . .}. Notice that the **union** of these two disjoint sets gives the set of all **natural numbers** (apart from 1 which is unique in having just one factor).

Rectangular 1. A rectangular **prism** is a prism whose **cross section** is a rectangle (same as a **cuboid**).

2. The x and y axes are said to be rectangular axes, being perpendicular to each other.

3. A rectangular **hyperbola** is one whose **asymptotes** are the x and y axes. The equation of a rectangular hyperbola is $xy = c^2$. See diagram over page.

Rectilinear Rectilinear motion is motion along a straight line.

Recurring A recurring **decimal** contains an infinitely repeating block of decimal **digits**. Examples:

$\frac{1}{6} = 0.16666\ldots$ written as $0.1\dot{6}$

$\frac{2}{11} = 0.181818\ldots$ written as $0.\dot{1}\dot{8}$

All recurring decimals represent **rational numbers**. Fractions with **denominators** containing prime **factors** other that 2 or 5 will recur if written in decimal form.

Re-entrant A **polygon** is said to be re-entrant if one or more of its angles is greater that 180° (i.e. a **reflex** angle).

this angle is — greater than 180°

Non-re-entrant polygons are called **convex**.

Reflection A reflection is a geometrical **transformation** of the plane in which points are mapped to **images** by folding along a *mirror line*.

this figure is called the mirror image of shape A

axis of reflection or mirror line

The object and image are **congruent**. A line joining any point P to its image P′ will always be **perpendicular** to the mirror line and the distances PQ and P′Q will be equal (see diagram above).

A **matrix** can be used to represent reflections in lines through the origin. Some of the simpler ones are given below:

Reflection in:

$$x\text{-axis } (y = 0) \qquad \begin{pmatrix} 1 & 0 \\ 0 & -1 \end{pmatrix}$$

$$y\text{-axis } (x = 0) \qquad \begin{pmatrix} -1 & 0 \\ 0 & 1 \end{pmatrix}$$

the line $y = x$ $\begin{pmatrix} 0 & 1 \\ 1 & 0 \end{pmatrix}$

the line $y = -x$ $\begin{pmatrix} 0 & -1 \\ -1 & 0 \end{pmatrix}$

Note: points on the mirror line do not change their position after the reflection.

Reflex A reflex angle is one that is greater than 180° but less than 360°.

Reflexive A **relation** defined on a **set** is said to be reflexive if every member of the set is related to itself.

Region A **network** divides the plane into regions. Regions are spaces enclosed by the **arcs** of the network.

this network has four regions including that 'outside' the network

The graph of a **linear** relation, for example, $x + y = 5$, divides the plane into two regions.

Each region can be specified by an ordering. In this case $x + y < 5$ and $x + y > 5$.

Regular A regular **polygon** is one having all its sides equal, and all its interior angles equal.

A regular triangle is called an **equilateral** triangle. A regular **quadrilateral** is a **square**.

a regular hexagon

A regular **polyhedron** is one in which all the faces are **congruent** regular polygons.

a regular **tetrahedron** is made up of four equilateral triangles

There are just five regular polyhedra: **tetrahedron, cube, octahedron, dodecahedron, icosahedron**.

Relation A relation is a connection between the members of a set, or between the members of two sets one to another. For example, 'is older than' on a set of people; 'is parallel to' on a set of lines.

Relations between two sets of numbers are of particular importance. For example: $x \rightarrow x^2 + 1$ between the set of all real numbers and $[1, \infty[$.

Remainder When 14 is divided by 4, the **quotient** is 3 (because $4 \times 3 = 12$) and there is a remainder of 2.

In any division process where the **dividend** is not a **multiple** of the **divisor**, there will be a remainder involved. For example:

$$362 \div 25 = 14, \text{ remainder } 12.$$

Note that $362 = (14 \times 25) + 12$, i.e., dividend = (quotient × divisor) + remainder.

The remainder theorem for **polynomials** states that when a polynomial P(x) is divided by $(x - a)$ the remainder is P(a). For example:

when $P(x) = x^2 + 7x + 2$ is divided by $(x + 3)$ the remainder is $P(-3) = (-3)^2 - (7 \times 3) + 2 = -10$.

Notice that if $(x - a)$ is a **factor** of P(x), then P(a) = 0. For example:

$(x - 2)$ is a factor of $P(x) = x^2 + 4x - 12$ and P(2) = 0.

Repeated root   If a root of an equation occurs more than once it is said to be a repeated or multiple root of the equation. For example, the expression:

$x^3 - 7x^2 + 16x - 12 = (x - 2)(x - 2)(x - 3)$.
Hence the equation $x^3 - 7x^2 + 16x - 12 = 0$ has three roots 2, 2 and 3. 2 is a repeated root.

Residue   When the numbers 8, 23, 38 etc. are divided by 5, they leave a **remainder** of 3, similarly 2, 17, 42, etc. leave a remainder of 2. We say that 8, 23, 38 all belong to the residue class $\bar{3}$ (**modulo** 5) and 2, 17, 42 belong to the residue class $\bar{2}$ (modulo 5). For modulo 5 there are five residue classes, denoted by $\bar{0}, \bar{1}, \bar{2}, \bar{3}, \bar{4}$ according to whether the remainder is 0, 1, 2, 3, 4.

Resolve   To resolve a **vector** in any particular direction is to find the **component** of the vector in the given direction.

The resolved part of the vector **d** in the x direction is vector **OB** and in the y direction is **OA**. The **magnitudes** are

$$|\mathbf{OB}| = |\mathbf{d}| \times \cos 40°$$
$$|\mathbf{OA}| = |\mathbf{d}| \times \sin 40°$$

The resolved part of the vector **r** in the direction **AB** has magnitude $|\mathbf{r}| \times \cos \theta$ where θ is the angle between the directions of **r** and **AB**.

Resultant The resultant of two or more **vectors**, is the single vector that would have the same effect as all the others combined.

The resultant is obtained by adding the **component** vectors.

186

Revolve   To **rotate** about an axis or point.

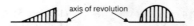

axis of revolution

If the shapes are rotated 360° about the axes marked, solids of revolution will be formed. The triangle will produce a **cone** and the semi-circle will produce a **sphere**.

Rhombus   A rhombus is a **parallelogram** with all of its sides equal. A rhombus has two lines of **symmetry** and rotational symmetry of **order** 2. The diagonals of a rhombus **bisect** each other at right angles, and bisect the figure.

Right angle   An angle equal to 90 **degrees**, or $\frac{\pi}{2}$ **radians**. It is a quarter of a full turn.

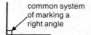

common system of marking a right angle

Roman numerals   A system of writing the **natural numbers** used by the Romans:

$$I = 1 \quad V = 5 \quad X = 10 \quad L = 50$$
$$C = 100 \quad D = 500 \quad M = 1000$$

All other numbers are made using combinations of the letters above:

4 = IV	(1 before 5)
6 = VI	(1 after 5)
27 = XXVII	(7 after 20)
90 = XC	(10 before 100)
1982 = MCMLXXXII	

Root A root of an **equation** is a value which when substituted into the equation in place of the unknown, will make the equation true. For example:

the roots of $x^2 - 7x + 12 = 0$ are 3 and 4
since $3^2 - 7 \times 3 + 12 = 0$
and $4^2 - 7 \times 4 + 12 = 0$

2 is not a root because $2^2 - 7 \times 2 + 12 \neq 0$.

A number is said to be a root of another if by taking **powers** of the number it is possible to make the other. Examples:

5 is the square root of 25 since 5×5 or $5^2 = 25$
2 is the cube root of 8 since 2×2 or $2^3 = 8$
3 is the fifth root of 243 since $3^5 = 243$

Rotation A rotation is a geometrical **transformation** where every point turns through the same angle. In a plane, rotation is about a single point called the centre of rotation. The centre of rotation is the only point which does not change its position after the rotation.

the rectangle has
rotated 90° about
the point 0

the triangle has rotated
90° about the point 0

To distinguish between **clockwise** and anti-clockwise rotations, + and − signs are used, − for clockwise and + for anticlockwise. For example, +60° means a rotation of 60° anticlockwise, −90° means a rotation of 90° clockwise.

Note that +90° = −270° and −100° = +260°, etc.

Rotations with centre (0,0) can be expressed in **matrix** form. For example:

$$+90° \text{ about } (0,0) = \begin{pmatrix} 0 & -1 \\ 1 & 0 \end{pmatrix}$$

$$-90° \text{ about } (0,0) = \begin{pmatrix} 0 & 1 \\ -1 & 0 \end{pmatrix}$$

An object can be rotated in space about an **axis** of rotation. For example, a **cone** is obtained by rotating an **isosceles** triangle about its axis of **symmetry**. See diagram over page.

189

Rotation of the triangle
gives a cone

axis   axis

Rounding off Rounding off is a way of **approximating** a number to a number with fewer non-zero **digits**. For example:

Round off £16.25 to the nearest £1 — £16
Round off 275 m to the nearest 100 m — 300 m
Round off 25471 to the nearest 1000 — 25000

When the first digit to be ignored is a 0, 1, 2, 3, 4, we 'round down'; when it is a 5, 6, 7, 8, 9 we 'round up'. For example:

273<u>8</u>1   to the nearest 100 is 27400   (round up)
42·<u>7</u>3   to the nearest 1 is 43   (round up)
6·1<u>2</u>38 is 6.1   (round down)
86<u>5</u>   to the nearest 10 is 870   (round up)
(The first digit being ignored is underlined.)

Row A list of numbers or letters written horizontally is known as a row. For example:

1 2 3 4 5 6

(2, 5) **coordinates** are written as a row

$\begin{pmatrix} 1 & 2 & 5 \\ 3 & 5 & 6 \end{pmatrix}$ this **matrix** has two rows

(1 7 6 4 2)   a matrix containing only one row is called a row matrix

Ruler A straight edge marked in linear units and used for measuring distances.

Sample A finite proportion of a **population** (which may be infinite). For example:

a sample from the set of **integers** could be 1, 3, 5, 7, 9, 11 or 1, 4, 9, 16, 25 or −1, −2, −3, −8, etc.

a sample from the letters in the alphabet could be {vowels} or {consonants}.

Satisfy 1. To fulfil the conditions of. For example:

120° satisfies the requirements of being an **obtuse** angle.

2. A value or set of values is said to satisfy an equation if, when they are **substituted** into the equation, they make the equation balance. For example:

$x = 3$ satisfies $x^2 + 5 = 14$ since $3^2 + 5 = 14$ is true.

$x = 2$, $y = 3$ satisfy the equations $x + y = 5$ and $2x - y = 1$ since $2 + 3 = 5$ and $2 \times 2 - 3 = 1$ are both true.

Scalar A scalar is a quantity that has size only but not direction (as opposed to a **vector** which has both size and direction). For example, time, distance, mass, volume are all scalars.

Scale 1. A series of marks on a ruler, measuring cylinder, etc., used as an aid in measuring distances, volumes etc. See diagrams opposite.

2. A scale drawing of an object has all measurements in the same **ratio** with the corresponding measurements of the original.

90 m 150 m
120 m

on a scale of
1 cm to 30 m
this becomes

3 cm 5 cm
4 cm

A map scale of 1:50,000 means that 1 cm on the map represents 50,000 cm − 0·5 km on the ground.

Scale factor When a shape is **enlarged** or reduced, the scale factor is defined as:

$$\frac{\text{distance between any two points on the image}}{\text{the corresponding distance on the object}}$$

$$\frac{A'B'}{AB} = \frac{A'C'}{AC} = \frac{B'C'}{BC} = \frac{3}{1}$$ so the scale factor is 3

193

If the areas of the shapes above were compared, the enlarged shape would have an area nine times larger than the original shape. We say that the area scale factor is nine.

If a solid shape is enlarged, for example, a **cuboid**, $2 \times 3 \times 4$ becomes a cuboid $4 \times 6 \times 8$, we notice that all linear measurements are doubled, all areas are multiplied by four and the volume is eight times larger. We say:

linear scale factor   = 2
area scale factor   = 4 (note $4 = 2^2$)
volume scale factor = 8 (note $8 = 2^3$)

Scalene   A scalene triangle is one where no two sides or angles are equal.

a scalene triangle may be right-angled

Scatter diagram A diagram showing the joint values of two variables.

	weight (kg)	height (cm)
A	75	60
B	60	51
C	65	58
D	90	60
E	62	55
F	80	55

Secant A **trigonometric** function. In a **right-angled** triangle the secant of an angle is the ratio:

$$\frac{\text{hypotenuse}}{\text{adjacent side}}$$

in the triangle ABC

$\sec \alpha = \dfrac{AC}{AB} = \dfrac{10}{8} = 1.25$

$\sec \alpha = \dfrac{1}{\cos \alpha}$

The value of α can be determined by examining a table of values for the secant function α = 36.9°.

Second 1. A unit of time. There are 60 seconds in 1 minute.

2. A unit of circular measure. Each one **degree** of angle can be subdivided into 60 minutes ($1° = 60'$) and each minute can be subdivided into 60 seconds ($1' = 60''$).

Section A cross section of a solid shape is a view of the shape taken **perpendicular** to its axis of **symmetry**.

the cross section of a cone is a circle

the cross section of this prism is an equilateral triangle

Sector A sector is part of a circle enclosed between two **radii**.

The area of a sector of $\theta° = \theta/360 \times \pi R^2$.

The arc length of a sector of $\theta°$ is $\theta/360 \times 2\pi R$ where R is the radius of the circle.

Segment A segment is part of a circle cut off by a **chord**. When the chord goes through the centre of the circle the two segments are called semi-circles.

Self-inverse A member of a set is said to be self-inverse if it combines with itself to give the **identity** element of the set under a given **operation**. For example:

the **matrix** $\begin{pmatrix} -1 & 0 \\ 0 & -1 \end{pmatrix}$ is self-inverse under matrix

multiplication since

$$\begin{pmatrix} -1 & 0 \\ 0 & -1 \end{pmatrix} \times \begin{pmatrix} -1 & 0 \\ 0 & -1 \end{pmatrix} = \begin{pmatrix} 1 & 0 \\ 0 & 1 \end{pmatrix}.$$

For example, the element 2 is self-inverse under addition **modulo** 4 since $2 + 2 = 0$.

Semi- **1.** A semi-circle is half a circle and is formed when a **chord** passes through the centre of a circle.

Area = $\frac{1}{2}\pi R^2$
length of semi circular arc = πR

2. The semi-**interquartile range** of a set of numbers is defined as: $\frac{1}{2}$ (upper quartile − lower quartile). For example, 1, 3, 7, 8, 9, 10, 12, 13, 17, 20, 27.

Upper quartile = 17 } semi-interquartile range
Lower quartile = 7 } = $\frac{1}{2}$ (17 − 7) = 5.

Sense Sense is a word used in connection with **transformations**. If the shape transformed is 'flipped over' by the transformation we say a change of sense has occurred. **Rotations, translations, enlargements** and **shears** do not change the sense of a shape, but **reflections** always do.

Sequence A set of quantities, often numbers, that are ordered a_1, a_2, a_3, . . . so that each member of the sequence corresponds to a particular **natural** number. Sequences are sometimes defined by a formula, for example, $a_n = 2n^2 - 1$ yields the sequence 1, 7, 17, ... Sequences can also be defined inductively by relating each term to its predecessors, for example, $a_n = 3a_{n-1} + 1$ and $a_1 = 1$ yields the sequence 1, 4, 13, 40 ...

Sequences can have a finite or infinite number of terms.

Series The sum of a finite or infinite number of terms, $a_1 + a_2 + a_3 + \ldots$

The study of a series and associated properties relating to **sums** and **limits** is an important branch of pure mathematics.

The sum to n terms of the series of terms in an **arithmetic progression** $a + (a + d) + (a + 2d) + (a + 3d) \ldots$ is:

$$\frac{n}{2}(2a + [n - 1]d).$$

The sum to n terms of the series of terms in a **geometric progression** $a + ar + ar^2 + ar^3 \ldots$ is:

$$\frac{a(1 - r^n)}{1 - r}.$$

Set A collection of distinct objects or things.

A set comprises **members** or **elements**, of which there may be a finite or infinite number.

The symbol { } means 'the set of', and the symbol ∈ means 'is a member of'.

Sets may be defined by listing or describing elements, and are often denoted by a capital letter. For example:

E = {even numbers} and 4 ∈ E

V = {a, e, i, o, u} and i ∈ V.

Sexagesimal A system related to a **base** of 60. For example, the common system of **degree** measure for angles is a sexagesimal system.

360 degrees = 1 revolution
60 minutes = 1 degree
60 seconds = 1 minute

Shear A transformation in which a line (in two dimensions), or a plane (in three dimensions) remains fixed whilst all other points move, **parallel** to the fixed line or plane, a distance proportional to their distance from the line or plane.

The area of a closed figure in a plane remains **invariant** under a shear. Likewise the volume of a solid remains invariant under a shear.

Shears with invariant lines or planes through the

origin of coordinates can be represented by **matrices**. For example:

$$\begin{pmatrix} 1 & 0 \\ 3 & 1 \end{pmatrix}$$

represents a shear in the x-y plane with the y-axis being held fixed.

Various geometrical and spatial properties of figures can be explored through the use of the shearing transformation.

The area of a **parallelogram** is equal to the area of a rectangle by a shear.

Side A side of a **polygon** is one of the line segments forming the boundary of the figure. For example, a **quadrilateral** has four sides.

Sieve (of Eratosthenes) An ancient process for finding **prime numbers** by striking out from the list of **natural numbers** firstly the multiples of 2 (4, 6, 8 . . .), then 3, then 5, etc., thus leaving the prime numbers.

Sigma A letter of the Greek alphabet. Upper case Σ and lower case σ.

The former of these two symbols is often used to signify a summation. For example:

$$\sum_1^5 a_i = a_1 + a_2 + a_3 + a_4 + a_5$$

$$\sum_1^4 i^2 = 1^2 + 2^2 + 3^2 + 4^2 = 30$$

The lower case symbol is often used to signify the **standard deviation** of a distribution in statistics.

Sign Notation used to signify whether a quantity is positive or negative. Positive sign $+$, negative sign $-$.

Also used in relation to the symbols representing various mathematical **operations** and relations. For example, multiplication sign $\times$, equals sign $=$, square root sign $\sqrt{\ }$.

Significant **1.** In **statistics**, a difference or deviation between observations and a proposed theory is called significant if it is unlikely to be the result of chance fluctuations.

2. The significance of a particular **digit** in a number is concerned with its relative size and importance in the number, and is dependent on the place value of the digit.

For example, in the number 39.08, 3 is the most significant digit, whilst 8 is the least significant.

Measurements are often **rounded off** to prescribed numbers of significant figures. For example, 27.058 can be rounded off thus:

> 30 to 1 significant figure
> 27 to 2 significant figures
> 27.1 to 3 significant figures, etc.

Similar Objects, plane or solid figures, are similar if they have the same shape.

When a shape is subject to an **enlargement**, the shape and its image are similar.

The corresponding angles contained in similar figures are equal, and the **ratio** of the lengths of corresponding sides of similar figures is constant.

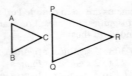

∠ BAC = ∠ QPR, ∠ ACB = ∠ PRQ, ∠ ABC = ∠ PQR
AB : PQ = BC : QR = CA : RP

Simple closed curve A curve that can be drawn with a single sweep of a pencil, with the end of the curve joined to the beginning, and such that the curve does not cross itself at any point.

Simple Harmonic Motion (SHM) The motion of a body that oscillates about a fixed point, its **acceleration** being directed towards the fixed point, and proportional to its distance from the point.

The time for a whole oscillation is called the **period** of the motion. The extreme distance from the centre is called the **amplitude**.

As Q moves round the circle, P moves along AB in SHM about O.

Motions of this type can be modelled by the projection onto a diameter of a particle moving with constant angular velocity ω round a circle.

Acceleration $= -\omega^2 x$

Distance from centre $x = a \cos(\omega t + \alpha)$

Period $= 2\pi/\omega$

Simplify To contract an expression by the use of algebraic or arithmetical techniques. For example $\frac{6}{9} = \frac{2}{3}$ or $3x + 2x + 4x = 9x$.

Simpson's Rule A method for finding the approximate values of definite **integrals**.

The method derives from dividing the interval over which the integral is defined into strips of equal width bounded above by **quadratic** curves, which are taken to approximate closely to the function being considered.

$y = f(x)$

The value of $\displaystyle\int_a^b f(x)\ dx$ given by Simpson's Rule with

$2n$ strips of width h is:

$$\frac{1}{3}h[y_0 + y_{2n}] + 4(y_1 + y_3 + \ldots) + 2(y_2 + y_4 + \ldots)]$$

For example, using the rule with four strips of unit width:

$$\int_1^5 x^3\,dx \simeq \frac{1}{3} \times 1 \times [(1 + 125\ ) + 4(8 + 64) + 2(27)]$$
$$\simeq \frac{468}{3}$$
$$\simeq 156$$

Simultaneous equations A system of several equations with several unknowns (often **linear**). Examples:

$$\left.\begin{array}{l} 3x + y = 17 \\ 2x - 3y = 12 \end{array}\right\} \quad \text{or} \quad \left.\begin{array}{l} x^2y + y^2 = 26 \\ x + y = 6 \end{array}\right\}$$

$$\left.\begin{array}{l} 3p + 2q + 5r = 6 \\ \text{or } 2p + 3q + 4r = 7 \\ 4p + 3q - 2r = 8 \end{array}\right\}$$

Linear simultaneous equations may be solved in a variety of ways:

(a) Substitution

$x + 3y = 11$
$5x - 2y = 4$

From the first equation $x = 11 - 3y$.
Substituting in the second equation gives:

$$\begin{aligned} 5(11 - 3y) - 2y &= 4 \\ 55 - 15y - 2y &= 4 \\ 17y &= 51 \\ y &= 3 \end{aligned}$$

$$\begin{aligned} \text{So, } x &= 11 - (3 \times 3) \\ x &= 2 \end{aligned}$$

(b) Graphical

$x + 3y = 11$
$5x - 2y = 4$

Draw the graphs of the two relationships.

The point of **intersection** of the lines (2, 3) gives the solution of the equations.

(c) Addition/subtraction of equations

$x + 3y = 11$
$5x - 2y = 4$

multiply the first equation by 5:

$5x + 15y = 55$

then subtract the second equation:

$17y = 51$
$y = 3$

now substitute to find x:

$x + 3 \times 3 = 11$
$x = 2$

(d) Matrices

The equations:

$x + 3y = 11$
$5x - 2y = 4$

208

can be written:

$$\begin{pmatrix} 1 & 3 \\ 5 & -2 \end{pmatrix} \begin{pmatrix} x \\ y \end{pmatrix} = \begin{pmatrix} 11 \\ 4 \end{pmatrix}$$

Applying the inverse **matrix**:

$$\frac{1}{17} \begin{pmatrix} 2 & 3 \\ 5 & -1 \end{pmatrix}$$

to each side of this matrix equation, we have:

$$\begin{pmatrix} 1 & 0 \\ 0 & 1 \end{pmatrix} \begin{pmatrix} x \\ y \end{pmatrix} = \frac{1}{17} \begin{pmatrix} 2 & 3 \\ 5 & -1 \end{pmatrix} \begin{pmatrix} 11 \\ 4 \end{pmatrix}$$

$$\Rightarrow \begin{pmatrix} x \\ y \end{pmatrix} = \begin{pmatrix} 2 \\ 3 \end{pmatrix}$$

Simultaneous equations arise from a variety of different physical situations, and the study of their solution forms an important branch of algebra. The idea of a matrix was developed through the study of equations of this type.

Sine A **trigonometric** function. In a **right-angled** triangle the sine of an angle is the ratio:

$$\frac{\text{opposite side}}{\text{hypotenuse}}$$

209

in the triangle ABC

$$\sin \theta = \frac{CB}{AC} = \frac{7}{25} = 0.28$$

The value of θ can now be determined by examination of a table of values of the sine function $\theta = 16.3°$.

in the triangle PQR

$$\sin 23° = \frac{PQ}{PR}$$

But from the table of values of the sine function $\sin 23° = 0.391$. Hence:

$$0.391 = \frac{PQ}{20}$$

and PQ = 7.82.

Singular A square **matrix** is singular if it has no inverse. For example:

$$\begin{pmatrix} 3 & 6 \\ 2 & 4 \end{pmatrix} \quad \text{or} \quad \begin{pmatrix} 2 & 1 & 3 \\ 1 & 4 & 5 \\ 4 & 9 & 13 \end{pmatrix} \quad \text{or} \quad \begin{pmatrix} 1 & 2 & 3 \\ 0 & 0 & 0 \\ 4 & 5 & 6 \end{pmatrix}$$

The **determinant** of a singular matrix is zero, and there are simple linear relationships between the **rows** of the matrix and between the **columns** of the matrix.

Singular matrices are associated with sets of **linear equations** without unique solutions. For example:

matrix $\begin{pmatrix} 3 & 6 \\ 2 & 4 \end{pmatrix}$

$\begin{aligned} 3x + 6y &= 9 \\ 2x + 4y &= 6 \end{aligned}$ $\begin{aligned} 3x + 6y &= 1 \\ 2x + 4y &= 7 \end{aligned}$

                 system with   system with
                 many solutions   no solutions

Skew lines Skew lines are non-**parallel**, non-**intersecting** lines.

In the diagram above, the line AB marking the boundary between floor and wall is skew to the line CD between wall and ceiling.

211

Skew distribution Data which when represented graphically produces a non-**symmetrical** profile.

The **bar chart** above represents the **frequencies** of various numbers of goals scored by soccer teams in a league.

The distribution is skew, the frequencies do not group around a central average.

Slant The distance l from the vertex of a right-**cone** to a point on the edge of the circular base, measured along the curved surface of the cone, is called the slant height of the cone. See **Cone**.

This measurement is used in calculating the area of the curved surface of a right cone. Area = $\pi r l$.

Slide rule A calculating aid looking similar to a simple rule, but containing a sliding **logarithmic** scale, which can be used to multiply, divide, extract roots, etc.

Slide rules were extensively used by engineers, draughtsmen and others involved in doing large numbers of calculations.

It has been largely replaced by the electronic calculator as a practical calculating aid.

Small circle A circle drawn on the surface of a **sphere**, whose centre does not coincide with the centre of the sphere.

The term is used most commonly with reference to the geometry of the earth. Lines of **latitude** are small circles (apart from the **equator**, which is a **great circle**) whose centres lie along a common diameter of the earth. See diagram over page.

small circles

Solid of revolution The solid formed by rotating a plane surface area through 360° about an axis.

Pictured above is the solid formed by rotating the area under the curve $y = f(x)$ between $x = a$ and $x = b$ about the x-axis. The flat area which sweeps out the solid is:

$$\int_a^b y\,dx$$

The surface area of the solid of revolution is:

$$\int_a^b 2\pi y \sqrt{1 + \left(\frac{dy}{dx}\right)^2}\ dx$$

The volume of the solid of revolution is:

$$\int_a^b \pi y^2 dx$$

Solution The process and result of solving a mathematical problem often in equation form. Examples:

The solution to $3x + 4 = x + 12$ is $x = 4$.

The solution to $dy/dx = x$ is $y = x^2/2 + A$.

The solution set to $x^2 \leqslant 4$ is the interval $[-2, 2]$.

Speed The speed of a body is the rate of distance travelled per unit of time.

Average speeds are calculated over a time interval by:

$$\frac{\text{distance travelled}}{\text{time taken}}$$

For example, an inter-city train travels 200 miles in $2\frac{1}{2}$ hours. Average speed:

$$\frac{200}{2\frac{1}{2}} = 80 \text{ miles per hour.}$$

The instantaneous speed of a body at a particular time is the **limit** of the average speeds over a **sequence** of time intervals that approach zero.

The graph above shows the distance travelled by a body in free fall.

The average speed over the second and third seconds is measured by the **gradient** of the **chord** AC. Averge speed:

$$\frac{45 - 5}{3 - 1} = 20 \text{ ms}^{-1}$$

The instantaneous speed after two seconds is measured by the gradient of the **tangent** at B. Speed:

$$\frac{40 - 20}{1} = 20 \text{ ms}^{-1}$$

Sphere A circular solid formed by the set of points in space all equidistant from a given fixed point.

A football, a soap bubble and a globe are all examples of roughly spherical shapes.

The fixed point is called the centre of the sphere, and the common distance of its surface points from the centre is called the radius.

The **Cartesian** equation of a sphere with centre at (a, b, c) and radius r is:

$$(x - a)^2 + (y - b)^2 + (z - c)^2 = r^2$$

The surface area of a sphere of radius r is given by the formula:

$$A = 4\pi r^2$$

The volume enclosed by a sphere of radius r is given by the formula:

$$V = \frac{4}{3}\pi r^3$$

Spiral A general term given to plane curves or curved surfaces with coils which resemble characteristic patterns found in the natural world.

sea shell

snail shell

spring

An example is the **logarithmic** or equiangular spiral.

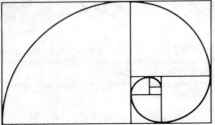

This spiral can be constructed by successive dissections of a rectangle into squares, and the **inscribing** of **quadrants** of circles.

Spread A term used to denote the dispersion of **data** from a measure of **average**. Two commonly used measures of spread are **interquartile range** and **standard deviation**. Examples:

Data A 19, 21, 15, 25, 20, 22, 18, 20, 17, 23
Data B 20, 0, 40, 30, 10, 5, 35, 2, 38, 20

The **means** of these two sets of data are both 20. However, the differences of the individual items of data from the means are:

For A 1, 1, 5, 5, 0, 2, 2, 0, 3, 3
For B 0, 20, 20, 10, 10, 15, 15, 18, 18, 0

The mean difference from the mean for A is $22/10 = 2.2$.

The mean difference from the mean for B is $126/10 = 12.6$.

Measured in this way the data in set B has a greater spread away from the mean.

Square 1. A square is a **quadrilateral** with four equal sides, whose interior angles are all 90°.

A square is **symmetrical** about its diagonals and the **perpendicular bisectors** of its sides, which are all **concurrent**.

A square has rotational **symmetry** of **order** 4.

2. To square a quantity is to multiply that quantity by itself. For example, 5 squared (written 5^2) = $5 \times 5 = 25$.

3. Square **centimetre** (cm^2), square metre (m^2), square **kilometre** (km^2) are all units used in measuring **area**.

A surface with area 5 cm^2, has the same area as five squares of side 1 cm.

Square root The number x is a square root of the number y ($x = \sqrt{y}$) if y is the square of x ($y = x^2$).

9 is a square root of 81 (written $\sqrt{81}$) since $81 = 9 \times 9$.

Positive **real numbers** have two square roots: for example, the square roots of 6.25 are $+\sqrt{6.25} = 2.5$ and $-\sqrt{6.25} = -2.5$.

220

Standard deviation A commonly used measure of the **spread** of individual items for **data** from the **mean** of the set of items. For example, the heights in centimetres of ten small plants are:

6.3, 5.9, 5.2, 7.1, 6.6, 6.8, 7.4, 5.3, 5.8, 5.6

The mean height is $62/10 = 6.2$ cm.

The deviations of each of the individual heights from the mean are:

+0.1, −0.3, −1.0, +0.9, +0.4, +0.6, +1.2, −0.9, −0.4, −0.6

The **squares** of these deviations are:

0.01, 0.09, 1.0, 0.81, 0.16, 0.36, 1.44, 0.81, 0.16, 0.36

The mean of these squares of the deviations is the **variance**:

$$\frac{5.2}{10} = 0.52.$$

The **square root** of this mean is 0.72.

This quantity, the root, mean, square, deviation from the mean is called the standard deviation.

The formula for calculating standard deviation is:

$$\sqrt{\frac{\sum\limits_{1}^{n} (x_i - \bar{x})^2}{n}}$$

for n items of data $x_1, x_2 \ldots$ with a mean of $\bar{x}$.

Standard index form A method of expressing numbers, popular in science and engineering, in which positive numbers are written in the form:

$$A \times 10^n$$

where $1 \leqslant A < 10$ and n is an **integer**.

For example:

$$734.6 = 7.346 \times 10^2$$
$$-0.0063 = -6.3 \times 10^{-3}$$

This notation is particularly useful for dealing with very large or small numbers.

Stationary point A function $y = f(x)$ has a stationary point at (a, b) if the **derivative** of $f(x)$ is zero at $x = a$, i.e., $f'(a) = 0$.

stationary points at $x=1$ and $x=3$

$$f(x) = x^3 - 6x^2 + 9x$$

The **gradient** of the graph of a function is zero at a stationary point and the **tangent** is **parallel** to the x-axis. Three types can be identified:

(a) *maximums*	
(b) *minimums*	
(c) *stationary inflections*	or

Statistics The study of methods of analysing large quantities of **data**.

The measures of the various properties of sets of data, for example, **means**, deviations, etc., are also known as statistics.

Subgroup A **group** H whose elements form a **subset** of a group G, and that shares the same **operation** with G is called a subgroup of G. For example:

The set {0, 1, 2, 3} under addition modulo 4 is a group

+	0	1	2	3
0	0	1	2	3
1	1	2	3	0
2	2	3	0	1
3	3	0	1	2

The subset {0, 2} under the same operation forms a subgroup

+	0	2
0	0	2
2	2	0

223

Subset If a **set** B comprises elements that are themselves **members** of another set A, B is called a subset of A (written B⊂A or A⊃B). All sets are subsets of a **universal set** ℰ. The **empty set** ∅ is a subset of every set.

If A contains **elements** not in B then B is a **proper** subset of A.

B⊂A

Substitution In mathematics, the replacement of one expression by another in order to **simplify** is known as substitution. The replacement of a variable by a number, for example, substituting $x = 3$ into the equation $y = 2x + 1$ gives $y = 2 \times 3 + 1 = 7$.

In particular, used as a method of simplifying certain **integrals**. For example:

In $\displaystyle\int \frac{1}{\sqrt{1 - x^2}} \, dx$ substitute $x = \sin \theta$

$$= \int \frac{1}{\sqrt{1 - \sin^2\theta}} \cos \theta \, d\theta$$

$$= \int 1 \, . d\theta = \theta + K$$
$$= \sin^{-1} x + K$$

Subtend An angle is subtended by an arc or line when the angle 'stands upon' the arc or line.

In the diagram below the arc AB subtends the angle φ at the **circumference** and the angle θ at the **centre**.

Subtraction One of the four basic operations of **arithmetic**. It is related to situations where one quantity is removed from another or when the difference between two quantities is to be calculated. Subtraction is the **inverse** operation to **addition**.

Sufficient Considering the statement 'if x is 3 and y is 4; then $x + y$ is 7', of the two conditions:

(1) 'x is 3 and y is 4'
(2) '$x + y$ is 7'

225

(1) is a sufficient condition for (2), i.e., if (1) is true, then (2) follows.

However, (2) is not a sufficient condition for (1), since if (2) is true (1) need not follow.

Sum The result of adding two or more quantities is called the sum of the quantities.

Supplementary Two angles whose sum is 180° are said to be supplementary.

angles standing on a
straight line
are supplementary

opposite angles in a
cyclic quadrilateral are
supplementary

Surd A surd is an expression involving unresolved **roots** of numbers. Examples:

$$\sqrt{2}, \sqrt{5} + \sqrt{7}, \sqrt[3]{8}, \sqrt{3} - \sqrt{2}, \text{ etc.}$$

Some expressions involving surds can be simplified. For example:

$$\sqrt{8} = \sqrt{4 \times 2} = \sqrt{4} \times \sqrt{2} = 2\sqrt{2}$$

Symbol A sign used to denote a quantity, operation, relation or other mathematical entity. Examples:

$$+ \quad \{ \} \quad \sqrt{} \quad \int \quad = \quad x$$

Symmetric A **relation** R on a set is symmetric if whenever aRb then bRa. For example, **congruence** is a symmetric relation on the set of triangles, but 'greater than' is not symmetric on the set of real numbers.

Symmetry Plane figures may exhibit two types of symmetry.

(a) **Line symmetry** The left-hand figure above is equally distributed about the two dotted lines of symmetry. It is unchanged by a reflection in one of these lines.

It has line symmetry of **order** 2.

(b) **Rotational symmetry** The right-hand figure on previous page maps onto itself under **rotations** of 120°, 240° and 360° about the centre point.

It has rotational symmetry of order 3.

Solid shapes may have symmetry about a plane, or about an **axis** of rotation.

Tangent **1.** A **trigonometric** function. In a **right-angled** triangle, the tangent of an angle is the ratio:

$$\frac{\text{opposite side}}{\text{adjacent side}}$$

in the triangle ABC

$$\tan\theta = \frac{AB}{BC} = \frac{3}{8} = 0.375$$

From a table of values of the tangent function the value of θ can be found: θ = 20.6°.

in triangle PQR

$$\tan 55° = \frac{QR}{6.2}$$

But from a table of values of the tangent function tan 55° = 1.43.

So $\frac{QR}{6.2}$ = 1.43 and QR = 6.2 × 1.43 = 8.87.

2. A tangent to a curve at a point is a straight line that touches the curve at that point, and has the same **gradient** as the curve at that point. If P has **coordinates** (a, b) and the gradient of the curve at P is m then the equation of the tangent at P is $y - b = m(x - a)$.

tangent at P

Terminating   A terminating decimal is one that has a finite number of decimal digits. For example, 0.41, 1.825, 0.1629385794.

All terminating decimals are equivalent to fractions having **denominators** whose **prime factors** are from the set $\{2, 5\}$. Examples:

$$\frac{3}{40} = 0.075 \quad \frac{7}{125} = 0.056 \quad \frac{13}{2000} = 0.065 \quad \text{etc.}$$

Tessellation   A regular pattern of tiles covering a surface is called a tessellation.

Tetrahedron A tetrahedron is a **polyhedron** with four triangular faces. A triangular-based **pyramid**.

Theorem A significant general conclusion obtained by logical deduction from certain assumptions called **hypotheses**, is called a theorem. For example, **Pythagoras' Theorem**.

Tonne A tonne is a unit of mass equivalent to 1000 kilograms.

this Land Rover has a mass of about one tonne

Topology The study of certain geometrical properties of figures that remain unchanged under particular types of **transformations**.

For simple plane **networks** properties such as the number and types of **nodes**, the number of **arcs**, etc., are topological properties which remain unchanged under the transformations considered.

Torus A torus is a doughnut-shaped surface.

It is the result of rotating in space a circle of radius *a*, about an axis in the plane of the circle, at a distance b from the centre of the circle.

The surface area $= 4\pi^2 ab$
The volume $= 2\pi^2 a^2 b$

Trajectory The path of a moving body, often used in the context of bodies moving under the influence of the earth's (or other large object's) gravitational field.

Transcendental **Irrational numbers** such as π (pi) and e, which cannot be obtained as the result of solving a **polynomial** equation with **rational coefficients** are called transcendental numbers.

Other numbers, including irrationals, which can result from solving such equations are called algebraic.

$x^2 = 2$ has $\sqrt{2}$ as a solution. Hence $\sqrt{2}$ is algebraic.

Transformation A change in spatial or algebraic work involving the **mapping** of one figure or space to another, or one expression to another, often by use of a **substitution**.

The study of various types of transformations, for example, **rotations**, **translations**, etc., is central to work in both algebra and geometry.

Transitive A **relation** R between **elements** of a **set** has the transitive property if it follows that when any three elements x, y and z are related xRy and yRz, then xRz. For example:

The relation $>$ ('is greater than') defined on the set of real numbers is transitive: $7 > 6$ and $6 > 4$ implies that $7 > 4$.

The relation $\uparrow$ ('is half of') defined on the set of real numbers is not transitive: $3 \uparrow 6$ and $6 \uparrow 12$ does not imply $3 \uparrow 12$.

Translation A geometrical **transformation** of the plane or of space of the form: $x \rightarrow x + a$, $y \rightarrow y + b$, $z \rightarrow z + c$, etc.

A translation is equivalent to referring to a set of new axes which are **parallel** to the original set.

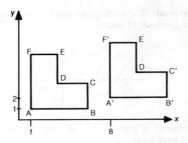

Translations are often written in **vector** form, in this case:

$$\begin{pmatrix} x \\ y \end{pmatrix} \rightarrow \begin{pmatrix} x \\ y \end{pmatrix} + \begin{pmatrix} 7 \\ 1 \end{pmatrix}$$

The image of a shape after a translation is **congruent** to the original shape.

Transpose The transpose M′ of a **matrix** M is obtained by interchanging the **rows** and **columns** of the matrix.

$$M = \begin{pmatrix} 3 & 1 \\ 2 & 4 \\ 6 & 5 \end{pmatrix} \quad M' = \begin{pmatrix} 3 & 2 & 6 \\ 1 & 4 & 5 \end{pmatrix}$$

Transversal The name given to a line that **intersects** with a given set of lines.

transversal

Trapezium A trapezium is a **quadrilateral** with one pair of **parallel** sides.

If the parallel sides are of lengths a and b, and are separated by a distance h, the area of the trapezium is A where:

$$A = \frac{(a + b) \times h}{2}$$

Tree diagram A diagram used to represent compound events and to enable their **probabilities** to be evaluated.

The tree diagram below represents the eight possible outcomes from tossing a fair coin three times.

The probabilities of individual events are marked on the appropriate branches of the tree, and the probability of a compound event such as getting a tail, followed by a head, followed by a tail, can be calculated by multiplying the probabilities along the branches.

Probability T, H, T = $\frac{1}{2} \times \frac{1}{2} \times \frac{1}{2} = \frac{1}{8}$.

Trial A trial is the repetition of a particular experiment under controlled conditions in a **statistical** investigation.

Triangle A triangle is a three-sided **polygon**. Triangles can be classified in a number of ways.

a scalene triangle has
no two sides equal

an isosceles triangle
has two equal sides
(and thus two equal
angles)

an equilateral triangle
has three equal sides
(and thus three equal
angles)

a right-angled triangle
contains an interior
angle equal to a right
angle

Trigonometry A branch of mathematics concerned,
at its simplest level, with the measurement of triangles.
Unknown angles or lengths are calculated by using
trigonometrical **ratios** such as **sine**, **cosine** and **tangent**.

Trigonometry also involves the study of the
properties of the various trigonometrical functions,
and their applications to the solutions of problems in
many branches of mathematics.

Trinomial Any **polynomial** with just three terms is called a trinomial. For example, $x^4 + x^2 - 5$ or $3x^2 + 4x + 1$.

Truncated A truncated **cone** or **prism** is produced from the original solid by removing portions with cutting planes as in the diagrams below.

truncated cone   truncated **cuboid**

Turning point A point on a graph, of a function, which is a local **maximum** or **minimum** value of the function.

At a turning point the value of the **derivative** of the function is zero.

turning points

Unbounded A **function** is unbounded over an **interval** if a value of the function can be found within the interval to exceed any given number however big.

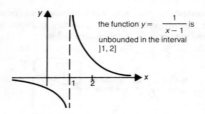

the function $y = \dfrac{1}{x-1}$ is unbounded in the interval $]1, 2]$

Unconditional An **inequality** such as $x - 1 < x$, which is true for all values of x, is called an unconditional inequality.

Union A **set** operation. The union of two sets A and B is the set of **elements** contained in A together with the elements contained in B. For example:

If A = {1, 2, 3, 4} and B = {3, 4, 5, 6}
The union of A and B is {1, 2, 3, 4, 5, 6}
The symbol $\cup$ is used to represent the operation.
Hence, A $\cup$ B = {1, 2, 3, 4, 5, 6}.

Units 1. The standard measures of mass, length, time, etc., are called units. For example, the **metre** is a unit of length, the **kilogram** is a unit of mass.

2. The term unit is also used to denote 1 or unity. For example, a 'circle of unit radius' is a circle of radius 1 of whatever unit is being employed.

Universal set The universal set, which is represented by the symbol $\mathcal{E}$, is the set containing all the **elements** of all the sets which are being considered in a problem. All sets are thus **subsets** of the universal set $\mathcal{E}$.

Upper bound An upper bound of a **set** of numbers is a number which no member of the set exceeds.

For the set of values of the function:

$$f(x) = \frac{3x - 1}{x}$$

with **domain** the set of positive real numbers, an upper bound is 3.

Value The **absolute** value, or **modulus**, of a **real number** is the positive numerical value of the number, ignoring any negative signs. The symbol for absolute value is | |. For example:

$$|-9.3| = 9.3 \qquad |7.2| = 7.2$$

The value of a **polynomial** for a particular number, is the numerical result of evaluating the polynomial with that number substituted in place of the **variable**. For example, the value of $4x^3 - 3x^2 + 7$ at $x = -2$ is -37.

Variable A quantity that can take on a range of values is called a variable. For a **function** $y = f(x)$, x is called the **independent** variable and can take on any value in the **domain** of the function. y is called the dependent variable and takes on values in the **range** of the function.

For example, for the function $y = \sin x$ the variable x can take on any real number value, whilst y can take on any value in the range $[-1, 1]$.

242

Variance For n items of **data** x_i with a **mean** of $\bar{x}$, the mean of the squares of the deviations of each x_i from the mean $\bar{x}$ is called the variance.

$$\text{Variance } \sigma^2 = \frac{\sum_{i=1}^{n} (x_i - \bar{x})^2}{n}$$

The **square root** of the variance $\sqrt{\sigma^2}$ is known as the **standard deviation**.

Vector A quantity that has properties of both **magnitude** and direction is called a vector quantity. Forces, **velocities**, **displacements**, etc., are vectors. The characteristic properties of vectors have been abstracted to produce a theory of vectors, which forms an important branch of pure and applied mathematics.

Vectors are often represented by directed line segments like **AB**, whose length and direction represent magnitude and direction. Vectors add up

around vector **polygons AB + BC + CD = AD**.
Vectors are often expressed in **component** form
relative to some standard basis,

$$\mathbf{AB} = \begin{pmatrix} 1 \\ 2 \end{pmatrix}$$ relative to the unit vectors along the

x- and y-axes.

The magnitude of **AB** is $\sqrt{1^2 + 2^2} = \sqrt{5}$ and its
direction is 63.4° to the x-axis $\left(\tan 63.4° = \dfrac{2}{1} \right)$.

Velocity Velocity is a measure of **speed** in a
particular direction. It is the rate of change of
displacement of a body per unit time. Velocity is a
vector quantity.

Venn diagram A diagram showing the relationships
between **sets**, by representing them as regions
enclosed by **simple closed curves**.

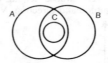

This Venn diagram represents the relationship
between the sets:

A = {1, 2, 3, 4, 5, 6}   B = {4, 5, 6, 7, 8}
C = {5, 6} where C = A ∩ B.

Vertex   In a **polygon** the point of **intersection** of two adjacent **sides** is called a vertex.

In a **polyhedron** it is the point of intersection of two **edges**.

Vertical   The direction **perpendicular** to the plane of the horizon is the vertical. In mathematics the term vertical is often used to denote measurements perpendicular to some defined base line. For example, the vertical height of a triangle.

Volume   The volume of a solid is a measure of the amount of space occupied by the solid.

The volumes of certain simple solids can be easily calculated.

cuboid
volume = l × b × h

prism
volume = A × h
(A is the
base area)

pyramid
volume = ⅓ × A × h
(A is the
base area)

Vulgar fraction A simple **fraction** with **integer numerator** and **denominator** is called a vulgar fraction. For example.

$$\frac{3}{4}, \quad \frac{23}{19}, \quad \frac{721}{859}.$$

Whole numbers The whole numbers or **integers** are the **positive** and **negative** counting numbers together with **zero**:

. . ., −5, −4, −3, −2, −1, 0, 1, 2, 3, 4, 5, . . .

Yard An imperial unit of length equal to three **feet**. There are 1760 yards in one **mile**.

Zero The **cardinal** number associated with the **empty set**. Zero is represented by the **number** 0 and is the **identity** element for addition: $x + 0 = x$ for any real number x.

Zone A zone is a **sphere** bounded by two **parallel** cutting planes.

The surface area of a zone of a sphere of radius r, produced by cutting planes distance h apart is:

$$2\pi rh$$